Southern Living®

COURTYARDS
To
COUNTRY
GARDENS

Southern Living®

COURTYARDS To COUNTRY GARDENS

TODD A. STEADMAN
with the Garden Staff of
Southern Living *Magazine*

MARK G. STITH
STEPHEN P. BENDER
LINDA ASKEY WEATHERS
RITA W. STRICKLAND
VAN CHAPLIN
SYLVIA MARTIN

Oxmoor House®

©1992 by Oxmoor House, Inc.
Book Division of Southern Progress Corporation
P.O. Box 2463
Birmingham, Alabama 35201

Library of Congress Catalog Card Number: 92-80927
ISBN: 0-8487-1015-0
Manufactured in the United States of America

FIRST EDITION

Editor-in-Chief: Nancy J. Fitzpatrick
Senior Homes Editor: Mary Kay Culpepper
Senior Editor, Editorial Services: Olivia Kindig Wells
Director of Manufacturing: Jerry Higdon
Art Director: James Boone

Courtyards to Country Gardens

EDITOR: REBECCA BRENNAN
DESIGNER: CYNTHIA R. COOPER
CONTRIBUTING WRITER: VICKI L. INGHAM
EDITORIAL ASSISTANTS: CATHERINE CORBETT,
TENA Z. PAYNE
PRODUCTION MANAGER: RICK LITTON
PRODUCTION: PAM BEASLEY BULLOCK

CONTENTS

INTRODUCTION

The South has a long heritage of garden design. It is evidenced by the formal courtyards of Charleston and Savannah, the vast lawns of plantation homes along River Road in Louisiana, and the simple country gardens of the rural South.

WHILE A LOT HAS CHANGED SINCE THESE traditions began, our love of gardening is still strong. The South is one of the most active gardening regions in the nation.

Perhaps the reason we are such active gardeners is as simple as a desire to hang on to our agrarian roots, even if the closest we get to farming is mowing a quarter-acre lot of St. Augustine grass with a riding mower. Maybe it is because we enjoy such a wide range of planting possibilities with our long growing season. Or perhaps it is simply that living in the South somehow brings us closer to nature. Speculation aside, the gardening tradition does live on in the land of magnolias and azaleas.

The gardens of today, however, are different from those of the past. Today's gardens are smaller. Lot sizes seem to be shrinking faster than house sizes, resulting in less outdoor living space and more carefully designed landscapes. In some ways, these smaller gardens exemplify the fact that our leisure time is at a premium. Despite the fact that we have smaller gardens and less time to work in them, the value we place on the landscape has significantly increased.

The reasons for gardening today are as varied as the individuals who garden. Perhaps the best reason of all is simply for the sheer joy of it—not only for the pleasure of designing outdoor space to suit your own personal needs and desires, but for the satisfaction of helping create that space yourself.

Chapter One
THE MASTER PLAN

All great gardens start with a master plan.

This plan is a comprehensive drawing of your future garden that shows the proposed project in its entirety. If you begin by developing a plan, everything you do, everything you plant, every structure you build will bring you closer to the garden of your dreams.

Secluded and tranquil, this garden provides its owners with their own little world—a place to dine, relax, entertain, or just get away from it all.

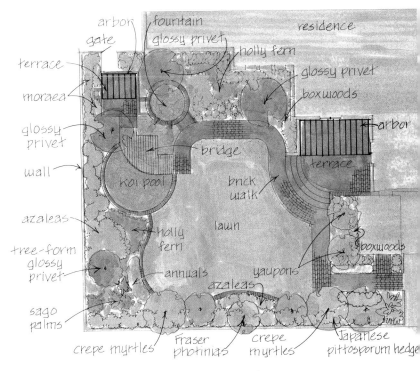

Viewed from the arbor (right), the family room and terrace seem deceptively far away. A curved wooden bridge, specified in the master plan (above), complements the arbor.

With an insightful master plan, natural beauty can still flourish.

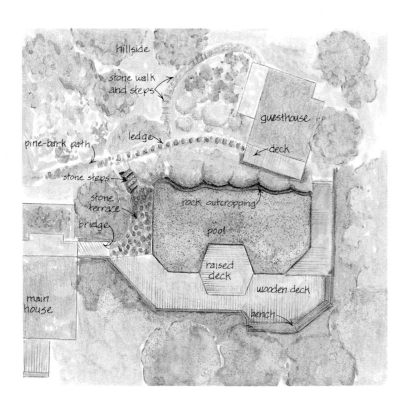

A stone path, winding between shade-tolerant plants, leads to the pool and deck. The bridge on the right takes you to the main house. A massive outcropping forms the pool's backbone (bottom left), while a hidden fountain sends water trickling over the rocks.

WORKING WITH PROFESSIONALS

While developing your master plan, if you feel that you are in unfamiliar territory, you may want to consult with a landscape architect or garden designer. Even if you plan to do it yourself, it often is helpful to seek advice at the beginning of the project. This is especially true if you have a vacant lot and plan on building a home. Consulting with a landscape architect before you break ground can save you time and money.

It is important to note the differences between a landscape architect and a landscape or garden designer. In most states, a landscape architect is required to be licensed. A landscape designer may or may not have formal training and in many cases does not have any practice or licensing restrictions.

Whether working with a professional or on your own, the process of designing a garden is the same. The first steps involve completing a site analysis and compiling a wish list of needs and desires for your garden. From that point, a series of drawings can be developed which will lead to a final design that includes construction drawings. With your master plan in hand, you can either do the work yourself or hire a landscape contractor.

SITE ANALYSIS

A site analysis is nothing more than a list of existing conditions. There are many ways to go about this, but the end result is a sketch of your property, as if viewed from overhead, that shows what you have on your site. Some information, such as the location of trees, steep slopes, and structures, is very tangible. Other aspects, such as views or privacy, are based on personal judgment. A site analysis should include anything that affects the experience of being in the garden.

Going through this process on your own is valuable, even if you plan to have your garden professionally designed. The more you know about your garden, the better equipped you will be to help someone else design the right garden for you.

The best way to get started is to relax in your garden on a sunny day and ponder your surroundings. It might be handy to have a notepad with you to record your observations. Let your imagination soar and try to visualize the garden you want. Get a feeling for the land, the wind, the pattern of the sun, and any noises you hear. Simply observe. Note what you like most and least about your piece of land. Your notes probably will read more like prose than a compilation of hard data, but this is a helpful step in getting a feel for your site.

If you plan to design the garden yourself, a site analysis is a must.

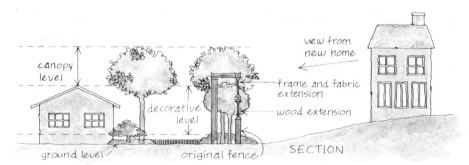

Changing conditions in your neighborhood can call for changes in your landscape plan. An existing fence was no longer tall enough for privacy when a new two-story house was built nearby (see section above). The creative solution (top) was to add fabric panels to increase the height of the fence. An arbor strengthens the taller fence visually and structurally.

Transforming a nondescript backyard into a spacious-feeling garden room starts with a master plan that helps you visualize the possibilities. A wooden deck and a terrace of pavers (bottom) now define living areas around a carpet of lush zoysia, which serves as a foil for the perennial beds.

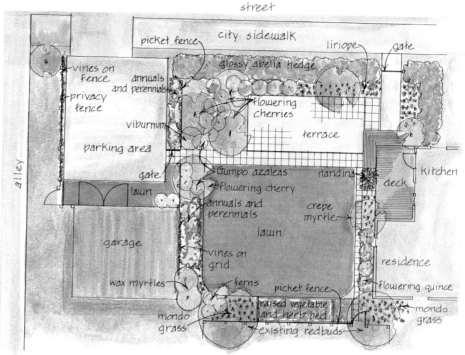

Correcting existing mistakes on the master plan helps you prioritize changes.

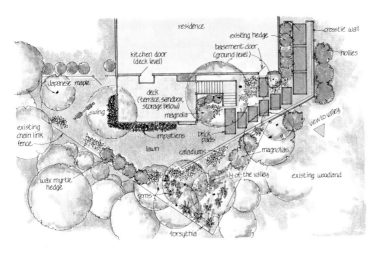

Originally, a second-story deck loomed over the neglected backyard (above). Lattice screened the space under the deck, making it a dark, useless cave, and the long flight of steps up to the deck was as inviting as an alpine climb. Now the area under the deck is divided into lattice-enclosed storage and a terrace (top). A quarter-turn in the flight of stairs (top left) inserts a pause in the ascent to the deck.

BASE MAP

Now it is time to set the notes aside and gather some specific information. The first thing you will need is a base map. This is a two-dimensional drawing that indicates your property lines and their relationship to your house. It should be drawn to scale and small enough to carry out into the garden. On it you will show all the physical features of the site as well as other pertinent information.

A plat (part of your mortgage papers) often shows lot dimensions and is a good place to begin. You can convert the plat to a base map by using graph paper. Most graph paper has ten squares to the inch and comes in a variety of sheet sizes. Pick a sheet size large enough to include all of your property, and plan on allowing each square to equal one foot (one inch equaling ten feet). If you have a large piece of property, you may have to let each square equal two feet or more. Start by drawing the property lines and indicating which direction is north. Make several copies of the base map.

Attach the base map to a clipboard, and tape a sheet of tracing paper over the base map for note taking. It will be useful to tape several layers of paper over the base map, then fold them back as you use them. Eventually you will compile the information from the various sheets into one comprehensive site analysis.

Having a 50- or 100-foot tape measure and someone to help you use it will make it a lot easier to take these measurements. You will also need some string and stakes to establish baselines for certain measurements.

With the property lines drawn, the next step is to show how the house sits on the lot. This requires a scale drawing of the floor plan of the house. Indicate the location of doors and windows and label the different rooms on the plan. This will help in designing entry areas and views into and out of windows. If your house has not been built, having a footprint of the house plan is useful in determining where you should build.

Starting at a known point, such as a curb or corner marker of the lot, measure the distance to several points on the house to determine where to place the outline on your base map. The more thorough and accurate you are at this stage, the better off you will be. Once the house is properly located, you can use it as a baseline.

Proceed with your drawing by indicating everything you have on your property. Be sure to show as accurately as possible the location and condition of all fixed or built structures such as garages, walkways, driveways, swimming pools, storage sheds, and anything else you consider permanent.

Determining A Baseline

One useful tip in locating features in the garden is the use of a baseline. A baseline can be established simply by running a string from one identifiable point to some other point in the garden, and then measuring off of that line. Draw corresponding lines on your base map.

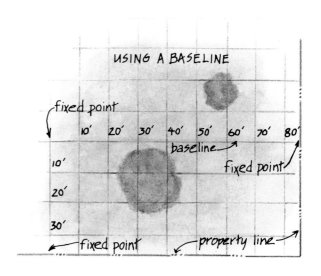

Vegetation and Soils

Locate all trees, shrubs, vines, lawn areas, ground covers, and flower beds. When doing this, estimate height and spread of the trees and shrubs as well as their condition. It is a good idea to determine the amount of upkeep required to sustain a plant, especially if you are concerned about the amount of time you spend on maintenance.

Any plant you already have or choose to add is only as good as the soil in which it grows, so you need to have the soil analyzed and amended if necessary. Soil sample kits, which are readily available from garden centers and county agents, will tell you about soil structure, pH, and whether or not you need to add nutrients. Carefully follow all instructions that come with the kit, making sure to take samples from various parts of the property since many lots have more than one type of soil. As you dig, pay attention to the depth of your topsoil and indicate any places where it is shallow.

Sun, Wind, and Rain

Your site analysis should include information on the effects of the sun, wind, and rain. Of course, you will need cooperation from the weather to record this. Don't worry if your neighbors think it is strange to be out walking in the garden on a rainy day, watching what happens to the water that falls. This information is very important for your analysis.

The sun patterns on your site dictate areas suitable for plants with specific light requirements. They also help you determine where to place landscape features, such as trees, pools, and terraces, to take advantage of or to avoid the sun. Knowledge of sun patterns can help you reduce heating and cooling costs as well.

Take note of where the sun rises and sets each day, structures or tall trees that block the sun, and patterns of shade created by your house. Keep in mind that southern and western exposures get the most sun and that if the sun is not shining through a window on a sunny summer day, it may shine through on a winter day. Try to estimate how the sun patterns will change throughout the seasons.

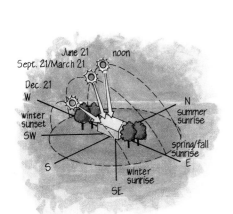

THE SUN'S SEASONAL PATH

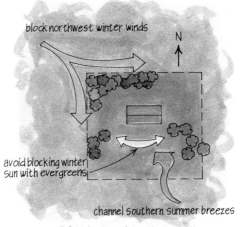

DIRECTING WINDS WITH PLANTS

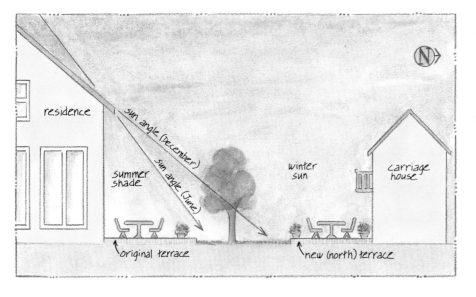

The wind is often overlooked in a site analysis. But anyone who has ever enjoyed a gentle breeze on an August afternoon can attest to its value. Likewise, a blustery winter wind pressing against a wall of glass can make you feel cold, even when sitting inside by the fire. Winds are fickle, but they tend to follow fairly regular patterns over the course of the seasons. Typically, summer winds come out of the southwest and winter winds from the northwest. Local geography can alter these general guidelines. Contacting a weather station, county agent, or consulting with neighbors will help you determine the direction of prevailing seasonal winds.

Knowing the amount of rainfall to expect is another important element in your site analysis. You need to anticipate the longest period of drought as well as the heaviest rainfall. Not only will this guide you in plant selection and the need to irrigate, it will help you decide if you have adequate drainage. Simply walking through the garden and looking for existing drainage channels is a good start. Be sure these features are added to the map, because if the pattern of drainage is altered by your design, you will need a new plan for runoff. The results of the soil analysis should also help determine potential drainage problems. For example, a hard-packed clay will not absorb water as readily as a sandy loam. Therefore, you may have more problems with drainage.

TOPOGRAPHY

One factor that affects how your site drains is topography. Note any steep slopes, sunken areas, rolling hills, or flat areas on the site. Indicate any extremes that exist, being sure to mark which is the top of the slope and which is the bottom. When it comes to designing the garden, you will need to be more specific about the actual percentages of slope. It is also a good idea to indicate the elevation of any structures. For example, show that the floor of the house is twelve inches above ground level or that the garage floor is below ground level, should that be the case.

DRAINAGE

Your garden needs to have an adequate drainage system in order to avoid potential problems such as dying plants, soggy areas, rotting wood, erosion, and mosquitoes. If you have any doubts about how well your site drains or how well your newly designed garden will drain, you may want to consult with a professional.

Many times you can solve a drainage problem by guiding water over the surface of the ground, either along existing drainage channels or new ones. Be careful not to divert water onto neighboring property; doing so is illegal in most cases. You may find you need to add a system of underground pipes that collect water and channel it to a sewer system, retention pond, or dry well. Even if it means a delay in building your garden, good drainage is an important step toward success.

A man-made stream bed of river rocks controls runoff during heavy rains and is an aesthetically pleasing, naturalistic feature when the weather is dry.

A narrow channel of stone between the raised walk and brick edging allows excess water to percolate into the soil instead of eroding it.

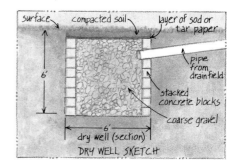

A Look At Legal Issues

Be sure to familiarize yourself with any local building ordinances, rights-of-way, easements, and setback regulations. This data identifies where you are and are not allowed to do any construction. More than once a well-designed fence has been torn down because the owners found out too late that it exceeded the legal height or was in a right-of-way. Your city hall should be able to give you this information if it is not indicated on your plat.

Locate all underground utilities as well as any obtrusive overhead lines. Most utility companies will locate the lines free of charge. This can save a lot of headaches further along in the design.

Site Amenities And Liabilities

Pay particular attention to the amenities on your site such as great views, nice trees, and secluded areas. At the same time, note any liabilities that need to be addressed, such as poor views, lack of privacy, and unsightly structures (whether on your property or neighboring land).

If you have yet to begin constructing your house, note the building sites that take advantage of amenities and require a minimum of earthwork and clearing.

A Look At The House

The last part of site analysis is the house. Make note of any areas that need attention. Entryways, windows, utility boxes, and air-conditioning units should all be shown. Also indicate any structural aspects of your house that will affect the garden, such as cantilevered roofs, high foundations, awnings, eaves, and steps.

Compiling The Data

After gathering your data, start with a fresh base map and put all the information together. If you have too much information to fit on one sheet, use two—one for vegetation, soils, structures, and setbacks; the other for views, wind, sun, and additional data.

Program Development

This part of the design process is where you determine your needs and desires as they relate to the garden. This "wish list" can be developed while you are doing the site analysis. To get started, simply gather the family and start talking. Write down everything that comes to mind, letting your imaginations run wild. Some things will be specific, such as a toolshed; other needs will be general, such as privacy. Obviously cost will have to be considered at some point, but don't concern yourself with prices now. You can make choices later.

Sample Wish List

- safety
- privacy
- parking
- a vegetable garden
- a play area
- an outdoor entertainment area
- a storage area
- a flower bed
- a barbecue area
- night lighting
- erosion control in an area
- a private/secluded garden
- a fountain

As you make the list, prioritize the items, because your wants and needs may conflict. Generally speaking, structural problems take precedence over embellishment.

As you develop your list, think about how you use your house and garden. Which entryways do you use most often? Do you cook out a lot? Where do the children play? How many cars do you need to be able to accommodate? Try to answer any questions you can think of that relate to how you use your outdoor property.

This is also the time to decide how much time or money you are willing to put into maintenance. You don't want to design and build a high-maintenance garden if you are not able to devote the time it takes to maintain it.

You also will need to make some decisions about quality and craftsmanship. As a general rule, it is better to wait to add any component of the garden until you are able to do it properly. Cutting corners when building a fence might provide privacy today, but it may need to be rebuilt in five years.

PUTTING THE PIECES TOGETHER

Now the real fun begins. You have a base map that indicates all of the opportunities your site presents, and you have a wish list of what you want your new garden to be. The next step pulls the two together.

Typically, each component of garden design fits into one of four activity areas: public areas (driveways, parking, front walk and entry, mailboxes); private areas (courtyards, terraces, decks); service areas (storage, utilities, outdoor grills, vegetable gardens); and recreation areas (swing sets, swimming pools, tennis courts, lawn areas). You can make your first diagrams on your base map by indicating which areas of the garden are best suited to your needs. For example, you may want to designate the entire front of the house as public space, a small area along the side of the house as service, the bulk of the backyard for recreation, with small pockets of private areas interspersed.

Once you have determined the use areas, move on to specifics and develop a conceptual design. Start with the high-priority items on your list, look at the base map, and see where they fit in. To help you get started, here is an example. Perhaps you want a play area for the children. If so, look at the site analysis to see where the children are currently playing and then look at areas that lend themselves to developing a new play area. When looking at the options, ask yourself: Is it safe? Can it be seen from the house? Is it big enough? You should have enough information from the analysis and program to eliminate a lot of possible locations, but there may be more than one suitable location. As you plug in all the various components, a logical location usually presents itself.

As you continue down your list, you may run out of space or find that the best locations are already taken. If this happens, simply draw another diagram. Continue in this manner until you have the most valued parts of the landscape indicated on the base map in locations that are suitable. You probably will not be able to include everything on your wish list. That is when you start making choices.

THE FINAL DESIGN

You are now at the end of the planning and the beginning of design. If you want to design your own garden, convert your conceptual diagrams into a preliminary design. To do this, start with a fresh base map and begin using actual or estimated dimensions of the various areas and features. This also is a good time to show your plan to a professional for recommendations and advice.

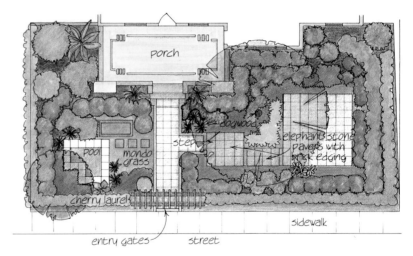

These diagrams (above and below) illustrate finalized master plan designs.

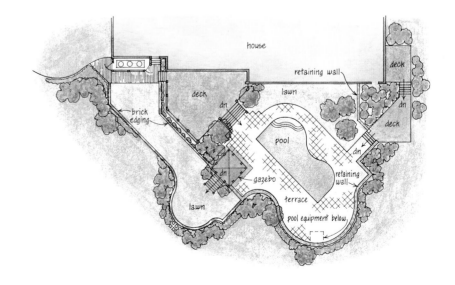

GARDEN DESIGN TOOLS

The tools of design can be broken down into two major categories: elements and principles. Elements can be considered the building blocks and includes line, color, texture, form, mass, and light. The elements of design are guided by principles: balance, emphasis, rhythm, contrast, scale, and unity.

Elements of Design

LINE

The line is one of the hardest working and most obvious design elements. Whether straight or curved, it is easy to identify and follow. A line draws the eye along to the desired destination. In the landscape, lines can be created by drives, walks, paths, the edge of a terrace, a planting bed, edging, or a fence.

Different lines evoke different responses. A vertical line leading away from you seems to draw you forward, while horizontal lines are more relaxing and tend to slow you down. Flowing lines are typically more relaxing than straight ones.

COLOR

Color is the most quickly noticed of the landscape elements. And because our eyes are naturally drawn to color, it is important to use it carefully.

Warm colors such as orange, red, and yellow, tend to advance and excite the eye. These colors are suggested when you want to draw attention to something, especially from a distance.

Cool colors such as greens and blues have just the opposite effect. They tend to recede into the background and have a soothing, calming effect. These colors are useful to help create the illusion of expanded space.

TEXTURE

Texture is generally broken down into three categories: fine, medium, and coarse. For plants, the different categories reflect the size, shape, number, and arrangement of the leaves. For example, the large, broad leaves of hosta are considered coarse textured, carpet bugleweed medium textured, and juniper fine textured. Paving materials and patterns, fence designs, and tree bark also represent texture in the garden.

MASS

Mass in the landscape design is formed by plantings of trees and shrubs. Not only are the plants important assets to the landscape, they provide one of the best ways of marking boundaries and separating one area of the garden from another. A mass of shrubs, such as a hedge, can create a natural screen. By contrast, mass defines open areas. Balancing mass with open areas is an effective way to add dramatic impact in the garden.

FORM

Form is the shape of a plant, plane, or object. When you look at a garden, forms abound—the rounded crown of water oak, the cone shape of a conifer, the boxiness of a deck. Forms add interest to the garden's design.

Different forms serve different purposes. Upright trees or structures generate awe: picture a piece of sculpture beneath a stand of upright trees. Geometric forms such as this hedge tease the eye and demonstrate control over the landscape.

LIGHT

Light is used in three basic ways in the landscape: back lighting, front lighting, and side lighting. Back lighting is at its best during sunrise and sunset when it silhouettes trees, shrubs, and structures of the garden, and random rays burst through to front light another part of the garden. Front lighting is useful for illuminating dark areas or to highlight a particular spot or object. Side lighting can be used to dramatically silhouette a plant or garden structure.

Principles of Design

EMPHASIS

The two guiding principles of emphasis are placement and contrast. Through placement and contrast the eye is drawn to a focal point. It may be a tree, a view, a fountain, or a piece of sculpture. Emphasis keeps us interested in the midst of monotony. For example, a row of boxwoods that is the same height can appear dull. Add to that row an upright plant in front of which is a birdbath, and you have created an interesting focal point which is enhanced by the row of boxwoods.

BALANCE

Balance in design is the same as balance in any situation. There is a certain peacefulness to a balanced garden. You achieve balance by manipulating elements such as color, form, and mass.

There are two basic types of balance: symmetrical and asymmetrical. Both depend on an imaginary or true axis (a line that divides the garden). Symmetrical balance means that what is found on one side of the axis is mirrored on the other. This is typical of formal gardens.

Asymmetrical balance also has an axis, but this time the components of each side are equal but not identical. A large plant on one side of the axis may be balanced by several small plants on the other side. You can balance a large mass on one side with a bright color on the other side.

SCALE

Proportion (the relationship between the size of any one plant or object and the garden as a whole) is how we gauge scale. This relationship is based on how we perceive space. The height of shrubs bordering a terrace is a good example. If the shrubs are only a foot high and the terrace is 15x30 feet, the shrubs will look out of proportion. On the other hand, if the shrubs loom fifteen feet overhead, they will be out of proportion.

RHYTHM

Rhythm and contrast are so intertwined that they should be considered together. Rhythm is the repeated use of a plant, color, form, or material. It helps simplify and unify the garden. Choosing plants with similar textures or colors is one of the best ways to use repetition in garden design.

CONTRAST

Often referred to as variety, contrast can be introduced as form, color, line, or texture. Like emphasis, it adds interest to the garden and prevents boredom. It provides the garden with highlights. Without contrast, one view in the garden would be the same as another.

UNITY

Unity is the harmonious combination of the elements and principles. There is no formula to determine when unity has been achieved. It is more of a perception. Examine each component of the landscape to see how it has applied the various principles and elements, and you can see how the different components of the garden relate to each other. In the end, you must decide if the design feels right. If it does, you have successfully unified the elements.

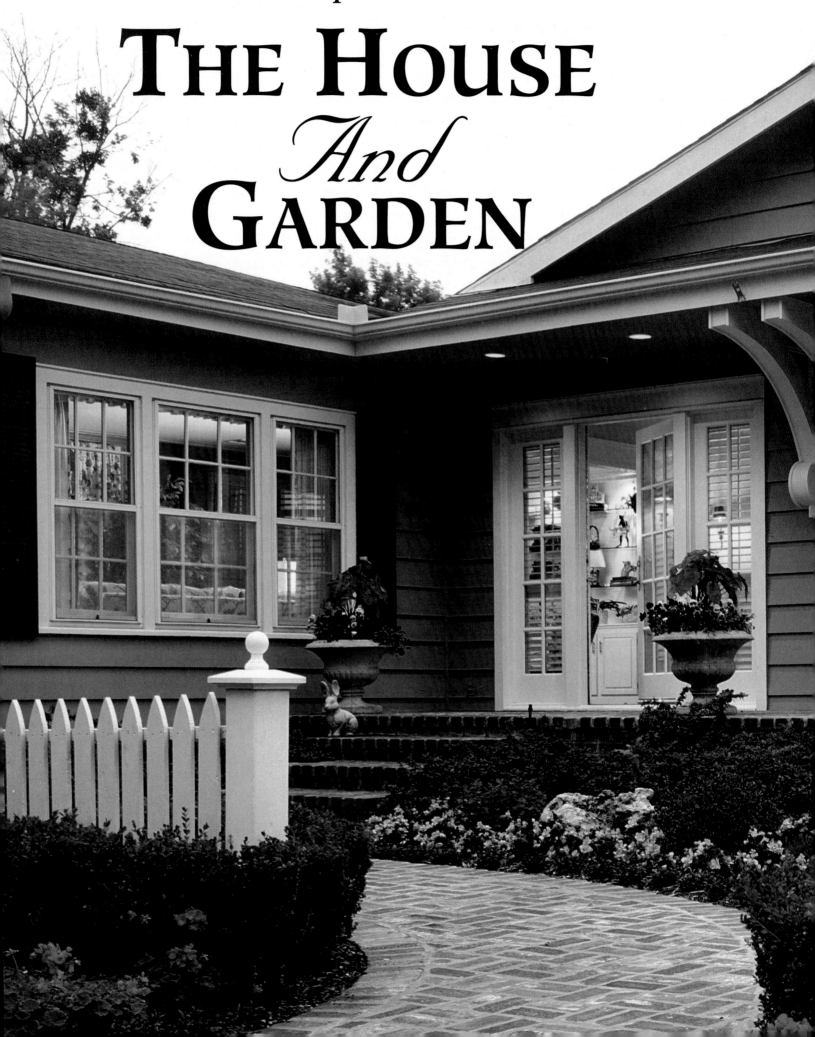

Chapter Two

THE HOUSE
AND
GARDEN

The statement your home makes about your style and taste affects the landscape, and your garden should reflect that style. Planning your garden with the look of your home in mind offers exciting opportunities to enhance both your house and garden.

... of dogwoods, azaleas, and common ... nes of the stucco house at left and link it ... ings. A broad flagstone walk that ... driveway to the front door offers a look ... h the setting and the stucco exterior.

Cash-for-Customers Drawing
$1,000 Monthly Voucher

Recipient's Name on Invoice

SUM *$1,000* **DOLS** **00** **CTS**

Pay To The Order Of

OXMOOR HOUSE guarantees to:

If your name is drawn,

Congratulations! Because you are a special customer of OXMOOR HOUSE, you have been automatically entered and have a chance to win in our Cash-for-Customers $1,000.00 Monthly Drawing. If your name is selected in this month's drawing, we'll send you a check for $1,000.00! It's that easy! Simply return your invoice today. (See back for details.)

Authorized by

OXMOOR HOUSE Controller

Keep this portion for your records.

BB-OX-FL-00/989

$1,000.00

Your home's landscape should express your personal style as well as that of the house.

Here, three houses that reflect historical styles are wedded to their settings by quite different kinds of landscapes, from simple, sweeping plantings to brick walls, paths, and benches that function as extensions of the architecture.

An apron of lawn spreading in front of this cozy bungalow creates the effect of a clearing in the woods. The lawn is in perfect scale with the house and provides a sense of presentation that plays up the entrance.

ENTRY GARDENS

Of all the points where the home and garden meet, the entry draws the most attention. This transitional space between the outside and the interior of the house conveys a lot about both your home and garden.

As proud homeowners, we want our guests to feel comfortable and welcome. Yet we sometimes forget that by the time visitors have crossed the threshold, they have already parked their car, walked to the door, and waited for their knock to be answered. If the parking was convenient, the walk pleasant, and the wait enjoyable, then the landscape has already extended a gracious welcome. The entry can set the tone for your landscape, whether it is a distinct and separate entry garden or a few carefully selected plants.

Entry gardens can be as varied in their style and detailing as the homes they serve, yet they all have one characteristic in common: They are set apart from the rest of the landscape. Regardless of how these spaces are formed—by walls, low hedges, fencing, or masses of shrubs—they give a sense of enclosure, a feeling of moving from one part of the residence into another. Whether as simple as a white picket fence framing a front lawn or as elaborate as a fully enclosed courtyard, entry gardens can be designed to complement any setting.

One of the main functions of an entry garden is to lead the way to the front door. However, an entry garden can also make a house seem more in scale with its surroundings. For example, a low garden wall can provide an intermediate step to smooth the transition visually between a two-story house and a level front lawn. On a sloping site, an attractively planted series of landings can move you comfortably towards the front door.

An entry garden should reach out to embrace you. Below, the gentle curve of a stone retaining wall draws visitors toward the front door. (Overleaf) Roses tumbling over a white picket fence express Southern hospitality with exquisite eloquence.

Shrubs with an open form accent the front door without hiding it. Strict symmetry here gives way to asymmetry in the placement of the terrace and stair, in response to the demands of the site.

ENTRY PLANTINGS

Whether or not you have an actual entry "garden," at some point you are confronted with the planting immediately around the front door. Because the entrance is where indoors and outdoors meet, it is a natural focal point for the garden. Use plants here that will draw attention to the doorway. Small trees and large shrubs are popular choices for entry plantings; just make sure that they are large enough to emphasize the doorway without overpowering it.

A flash of autumn color or a burst of springtime bloom can showcase your entry, but do not rely on seasonal color alone. For an attractive entry garden, you need year-round focus, so choose plants with special characteristics that will transcend the seasons.

Shrubs or small trees with intriguing shapes are excellent for accenting the entrance. Crepe myrtles offer sculptural trunks, bright autumn foliage, and summer blooms. Waxleaf privet grows rapidly and well in most of the South and can be easily limbed up for a multi-stemmed effect. Its

rich evergreen foliage offers a welcome sight all year long. Another excellent evergreen for use as a tree-form accent is the native yaupon. You might also consider a sweet bay magnolia. If you do not plan to use your plants as tree-form specimens, remember to allow enough room for them to reach their full, mature shape. Otherwise, they may eventually block the entry.

Plants with eyecatching details, such as the peeling bark of river birch or the blooms of flowering dogwood, add a nice element of interest. Delicate foliage also enhances an entry planting. Avoid using plants with thorny leaves and stems that could grab you or your guests as you come and go.

Architectural style plays an important role in selecting the

right plant. A formal home might call for matched plantings balancing the entry, while more contemporary designs provide the chance to use an asymmetrical arrangement.

If you enter your home from a terrace, courtyard, or deck, you can still enjoy the benefits of an accent plant. Just select a container and plant that are appropriate to the style of your house.

Shrubs may be the backbone of an entry planting, but in this courtyard entrance, it's the pots, planters, and lush, low beds that greet the eye with cool greens and blues and lively reds.

With container plants, you can change the look of your entry garden to reflect the seasons. A narrow front yard (left) is planted in a uniform way, and pots of plants provide the exclamation points of color. Below, large pots of wax begonias balance a tree-form shrub beside the door.

Choose containers as you would accessories for your living room: make sure the materials, colors, and shapes harmonize with your home's facade.

Standards in concrete planters match the graceful formality of the Federal-style door (left). Large terra-cotta pots complement the warm reds in the door and brick porch (above). Similar pots suit the textures of stone and stucco (right); the plantings repeat those in the beds for a unified effect.

Benches, lampposts, and awnings are both practical and welcoming. A bench may be a focal point (above) that beckons or a handy place to put packages while you unlock the door (opposite top). Awnings shelter you from the weather and add character to a porchless facade.

WHERE THE HOUSE AND GARDEN MEET

After your guests have strolled through your entry garden and arrived at your door, there still are a few finishing touches that will ensure that the transition from the garden to the house is a safe and attractive one.

Extending an eave or adding an awning will protect your family and guests from rain while the door is being opened. Evaluate the door itself and how it matches the rest of the architecture. The front door can be an exciting accent for the front of your house. You may consider adding a bench or seat by your doorway as a place to prop packages or as a nice spot to sit and enjoy the garden. You may also want to reconsider your outdoor lighting. In addition to providing safety, lighting can introduce a new look to your home's exterior.

Awnings add color and dimension, emphasize architectural details, and offer protection from the weather. Awnings keep direct sun rays from coming into the interior, so your house will be cooler.

ADDING AN AWNING

There are no standard sizes for awnings, but they can be cut to fit almost any door or window. The cost of an awning depends on its size, shape, and the fabric used.

For windows, there are four basic awning designs: the familiar square awning or standard installation, the Venetian awning, the hideaway or roll-type awning, and the circular awning.

Door awnings fall into two main categories: the circular style, which caps a door with either square or round shapes, and the Venetian style, which is the same for both doors and windows.

Awnings used to cover a deck or terrace are called canopies.

With this type of use, the highly visible underside of the fabric can be as important as the top, so choose your fabric carefully, perhaps using a material printed on both sides.

TIPS ON CARE
The life and good looks of your awnings depend a great deal on the way you care for them. Even awnings made from the finest materials with long warranties need a certain amount of care.
- Keep your awnings clean. This is the best protection from mildew. Even on mildew-resistant fabrics, mildew can grow on accumulated dirt or foreign materials and will eventually stain or damage the fabric.
- Keep shrubbery and vines away from the awnings, since many plants contain an acid that may be harmful to the material.
- Standing water on your awnings may cause pocketing or stretching, so keep excess water brushed off.
- Don't use a charcoal grill underneath an awning. The smoke from the grill will get into the fabric and may cause graying of colors.
- Folding or rolling your awning in extremely cold weather could cause cracking of the finish. If they must be taken down, store them flat until temperatures are warmer.

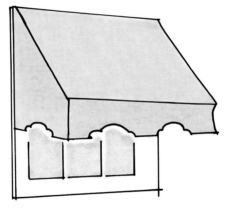

The familiar square awning, known as a conventional or standard installation, fits the basic shape of either windows or doors.

The circular awning follows the arched shape of either windows or doors.

The Venetian awning slants outward from the house and is held up by bars with decorative tips.

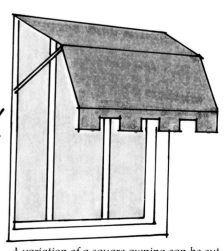

A variation of a square awning can be cut and fitted over casement windows.

LIGHTING THE ENTRY

Though every house is different, there are two types of lighting which are generally considered to be best for a safe and attractive entrance: decorative lighting beside the door and a downlight above the door.

If the entry has a high ceiling, the overhead light can be a hanging fixture such as a lantern or globe. In most cases, however, a recessed light or surface-mounted can light works best. The downlight not only lights the door but creates a warmer welcome once the door is opened, since it lights the person in the doorway. From a distance, a recessed overhead light cannot be seen, giving the illusion that the decorative fixtures alone light the door.

Avoid overlighting the door. The eyes of a person approaching the house will be adjusted to darkness, so a light that is too bright will be uncomfortable. An overhead light that is too bright can also overpower a decorative wall light, especially one that is designed to cast an attractive pattern of light and shadow.

You can adjust the brightness of your outdoor lights with dimmer switches, but it is better to adjust the wattage of the bulbs to a pleasing level of light instead, as dimmers can easily be turned off or altered by mistake.

A downlight above the door bathes both you and your visitors in soft illumination. Decorative lanterns on either side of the door (right) create a warm, inviting glow.

Well-chosen shrubs and small trees at the foundation knit a house into the landscape, softening the contrast between architecture and nature. When the foundation planting is done properly, the house merges seamlessly with its setting.

FOUNDATION PLANTINGS

Foundation planting refers to the plants that are next to the house. Their purpose is to help balance the architecture and tie the house to the garden.

Foundation plants can be used to emphasize or highlight the architecture. For instance, you can complement the formal, symmetrical design of a house by using a formal, symmetrical planting. This does not mean a clipped row of identical shrubs. Instead, balance the front of the house with groupings of shrubs on each side. If you have a cluster of dwarf yaupon to the left of an entry, you might want a similar cluster on the right.

An asymmetrical house can have its irregular shape highlighted by loosely arranged clusters of plants along the base of the house. A large planting can be used on one side of the house to create a pleasing balance with a garage or prominent architectural feature on the other side.

A foundation planting can also draw attention to a specific feature, such as a front door or bay window. In this way, the plants serve as an exclamation point. Crepe myrtles, flowering dogwoods, and Japanese maples are a few good examples of small trees that call attention to an area; in most cases, they will not grow to an overwhelming size.

A more practical use of foundation plantings is to mask or hide unsightly features such as meters,

vents, or the foundation itself, which may detract from the overall appearance of the house.

Be aware of the growth habits of the plants you use in your foundation planting. Many times the character of an individual shrub is lost in an overgrown mass. To enable plants to reach their mature size and still maintain a normal form, make sure there is enough room between individual plants and also between the plants and the house. Massing a lot of young shrubs too close together may give a finished look now, but in a few years the planting will be overcrowded.

Avoid using a hedge of shrubs around the base of the house. This treatment separates the house from the landscape and makes it appear to float above the garden. In most cases, planting beds should have form and movement instead of being static. If a straight row is called for, use plants of similar shape and color

and let them grow into their natural forms. The different textures will create interest and avoid monotony.

For variation and seasonal interest, consider using evergreen and deciduous plants together. Be sure to limit the number of different types of plants to prevent the design from becoming confusing or distracting.

Using plants of various sizes is another way to break up a boring look. Certain selections of azalea, juniper, boxwood, barberry, and other slow-growing shrubs offer a wide range of sizes and forms. If you have a low porch or window, you may prefer a ground cover such as mondo grass, liriope, or Japanese star jasmine.

As you plan your foundation planting, pay attention to the rest of the garden. You may want to use this area as an opportunity to repeat plants used in other parts of the garden, thus unifying the overall garden design.

Evergreen shrubs and jasmine follow the zigzagging path of the entrance walk (above). Against this foundation planting, crepe myrtles rise like living sculpture. Flowers and low-growing shrubs make a carpet of color and texture that frames the entrance and softens the look of the stone facade (below).

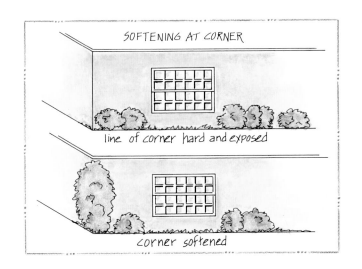

SOFTENING AT CORNER

line of corner hard and exposed

corner softened

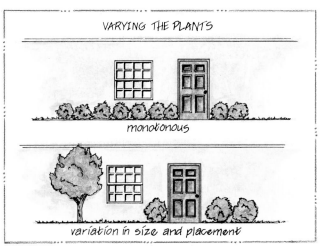

VARYING THE PLANTS

monotonous

variation in size and placement

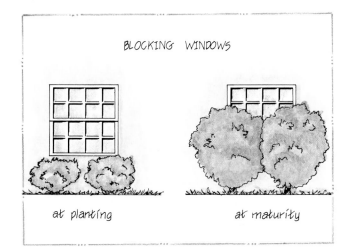

BLOCKING WINDOWS

at planting

at maturity

PLANTING AROUND THE ENTRY

at maturity

Enclosed by a white picket fence, the front yard becomes an informal entry garden. Instead of lawn grass, a perennial bed fills one half of the yard, and a curving brick path leads guests to the front door.

Though a new foundation planting (left) will look sparse, it is important to allow room for shrubs to reach their mature size.

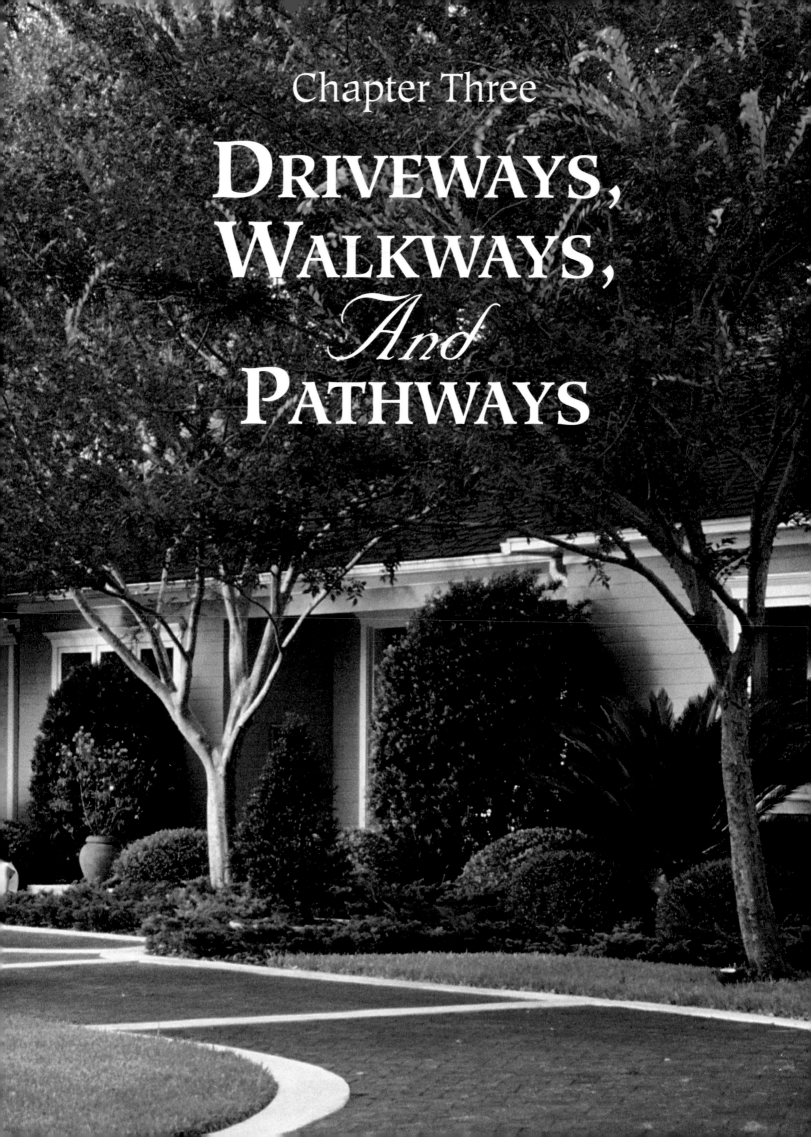

Chapter Three

DRIVEWAYS, WALKWAYS, AND PATHWAYS

Driveways, front walks, and garden paths serve practical purposes, but with a little planning, they can also create a charming ambience and dramatically showcase your garden. Drives and walks form strong lines and delineate distinct areas of the garden, so they are useful design tools as well.

A straight driveway located on one side of the property is practical and unobtrusive, leaving most of the yard free for the garden.

DRIVEWAYS AND PARKING AREAS

THE DRIVEWAY

Your driveway should be clearly indicated from the street, and it should be wide enough for a car to maneuver comfortably. In addition, you need to have ample and logical parking. It also helps to have some landmark, such as a mailbox, planting, or light, to clearly show where your driveway begins. Be sure that anything planted or constructed near the curb does not obstruct the driver's view of oncoming traffic.

If your driveway leads directly to a garage or carport, you may want to consider a turnaround, which will allow you to reverse directions and drive out forward rather than backing into traffic. A turnaround can also serve as parking space.

A long driveway gains added interest when curves are introduced. Curves should mold to the existing landscape as well as possible, and they should be bold enough to be easily negotiated.

Circular drives pose special challenges. When planned properly, circular drives can be quite stately, but they do require a lot of space. For a full-size car to have room to turn, a twenty-foot turning radius is recommended, though a larger turning radius is more comfortable for most drivers. If a circular drive has a parking area near the front door, the drive needs to be at least eighteen feet to allow for passage around parked cars. Remember that a circular drive places cars directly in front of the house, which may detract from the view.

If you have a steep site, you may need to angle the drive across your property to maintain a safe grade. Driveways on steep slopes will also require a level transition area of twelve feet or more where the drive meets the parking area as well as where it meets the street.

Your driveway should have a width of ten feet for a single lane of traffic, but to allow for easy passing of parked cars, a two-lane drive should be at least eighteen feet wide. Twenty feet is better.

The construction materials for driveways vary depending upon the expected use of the drive, existing materials in the landscape, and your budget. Asphalt, concrete, and gravel are commonly used and can easily accommodate most traffic. On the other hand, if large delivery and utility trucks will be using the drive, you may need to establish a stronger than usual roadbed.

PARKING

The following is a checklist of general guidelines to determine if your existing parking needs are being met. If any of these situations apply to your home, you may want to consider making some changes in your parking.
- All of your cars are parked and one cannot be moved without shifting the others.
- Visitors regularly use the wrong entrance.
- People are frequently forced to park on the street.
- You have to back out over fifty feet to reach the street.
- You consistently back over plants or the lawn when making basic driveway maneuvers.

CURBSIDE PARKING

With curbside parking, the pavement of the parking area joins the pavement of the street. Visitors pull directly into the space, parking either parallel or perpendicular to the street. This solves the problem of guests knowing where to park as it is

The parking area for most homes will fall into one of two main categories: curbside parking or on-site parking.

usually easy to spot. Curbside parking should definitely be considered if you have a small or steeply sloped lot.

Before planning curbside parking, check any zoning restrictions or regulations that may govern this type of construction. In most cases, you will need to have a building permit.

Parallel curbside parking requires a minimum width of nine feet to allow cars to park and passengers to get out of the car safely. You need to allow twenty-two feet in length for each car. This type of parking is useful particularly if you have a steep slope that would require grading and a retaining wall in order to add on-site parking.

Perpendicular parking offers greater protection for the visitor and the car. One drawback, however, is that it will require the driver to back out onto the street when leaving. If you have a perpendicular parking area, be sure the driver's view remains unobstructed.

Spaces for perpendicular parking should be a minimum of nine feet wide and twenty-two feet long. If there is a walkway along the parking area, you will need to add a wheelstop to prevent the front end of the car from blocking the walk, or you will need to make the walk wider.

A circular drive (above left) requires a lot of space but makes a grand approach to a stately home. On a small lot (above), the simplest solution is off-street parking that lets you pull straight in. Paving the drive with bricks links it visually to the raised planters and sidewalk so that it seems more like a terrace than a parking pad.

A parking area perpendicular to the drive allows you to back up and turn around in the driveway instead of having to back out into a busy street.

ON-SITE PARKING

If space allows, on-site parking is preferred to curbside parking. The shape and location of your driveway, the amount of space you have to work with, and the slope of your property are important considerations when deciding where to locate your on-site parking.

The parking area should be as close to your home's entry as possible. Of course, this area should not detract from the overall look of the landscape, so you should avoid locating the parking area directly in front of the house. Using existing level areas will reduce the cost and trouble of adding parking. Just be sure to allow enough space to maneuver easily into and out of the parking spaces.

Choices for on-site parking include perpendicular parking, parallel parking, and angled parking. If the driveway dead-ends near the house, perpendicular parking may be best. This allows drivers to back up and turn around in the driveway rather than into a busy street. When laying out a ninety-degree parking court, be sure that the turning radius can be negotiated easily. Consider fifteen feet as an absolute minimum with twenty feet preferred. As with curbside parking, use a wheelstop if a walkway goes along the front edge of the parking area.

Parallel parking is especially useful on narrow lots or when only one or two spaces are needed. Again, backing into the street may be a problem unless a turnaround area is provided. If only one parking space is needed parallel to the drive, a length of twenty feet is adequate. Increase the length to twenty-two feet per space if two or more spaces are required. For angled or perpendicular parking, plan on twenty feet. Always allow a width of at least nine feet for each space.

Parking bays set at a thirty- or sixty-degree angle to the drive are the easiest to pull into or back out from, but they take up the greatest amount of space. Also consider that the width of most driveways makes turning around after backing out of the bay fairly difficult.

With the right materials, a parking court can be a tremendous asset to your landscape. Though many people reject the idea of paving too much of their front yard, a parking court can take care of parking needs attractively and can serve equally well as an area for entertaining.

Finally, consider water runoff and drainage. An impermeable surface, such as concrete or asphalt, is going to increase the amount of runoff you have. Be sure that the water falling or draining onto the driveway and parking area is channeled to a collection point that feeds into a city sewer or drainage area. It may be necessary to have more than one collection point along a drive to avoid having a stream running down it during a heavy rain. As a general rule, you are responsible for the water that drains off of your property, so by adding a considerable amount of paving, and thereby increasing the amount of water that runs off of your property, you may create problems for your neighbors. This issue may be addressed best by a professional designer or contractor.

Minimum Critical Dimensions For Parking

- straight drive: 9 feet wide
- curved drive: 11 feet wide
- two-way drive: 16 feet wide
- straight drive with parallel parking: 18 feet wide
- parking place: 9 feet wide
- parallel parking place: 22 feet long
- perpendicular parking place: 22 feet long
- backing-out room for perpendicular parking: 32 feet
- turning radius: 20 feet

Walkways And Pathways

Whether it is a stamped concrete walk from the parking area to the front door or a meandering stone path through a bed of wildflowers, strolling through the garden gives great pleasure. When deciding where to place a walk in your garden, be sure to consider more than just getting from one place to the next. Like driveways, the strong lines formed by walkways delineate space. They also help create planting beds and can organize your landscape into different use areas.

The Front Walk

When bringing guests from the street or parking area to your front door, you need to provide a comfortable transition. A landing near the parking area gives people room to get out of their cars and directs them onto the walkway. The walk to the front door should be wide enough to accommodate two adults walking side-by-side. Consider four feet as a minimum. A six-foot width is even more comfortable, but may take up more room than you have to spare. Regardless, the width should bear a relationship to the length. For example, in most cases a long walk should be wider than a short one.

Stamped concrete gives you the look of stone paving without the expense. Positioning the pattern on the diagonal subtly points visitors toward the door.

Many times a front walk is straight because it is the shortest distance between the street and the front door. However, such a direct approach can be uninteresting. A few design ideas can help make the walk more attractive, whether curved or straight.

Contrasting materials of slate and brick and attention to proportions make the walk (left) visually pleasing. Using the same materials on the porch and the landing provides a smooth transition from the walk to the street. This gives the whole promenade a unified effect. Curbside plantings (below) frame the entrance to the walk and help downplay its length.

A walkway shaped around existing planting beds results in a more interesting approach to the house. Here, the walk zigzags around established beds, each of which features a sculptural tree. The design of the walk, as a raised wooden platform, plays off of the vertical boarding of the house, and its graphic lines express the same contemporary feeling.

Emphasize the lines of your walkways with plantings. Be bold with this approach. If the walk is narrow, plant a strip of ground cover at least twice its width on each side. Edging the walkway with thin strips of ground cover will only cause the walk to look more narrow, an effect you don't want.

Plant a series of beds along the walk to create a dynamic look. You have a captive audience as guests walk toward your front door, so treat them to different views. Let the planting beds come to the edge of the walk or even creep onto the walk itself to create the sensation of strolling through a garden on the way to the house. You can also try using pavers or

stepping stones as a means of slowing the approach, which allows guests time to take in the surrounding landscape.

A broad landing at the head of the walk allows you to introduce an intriguing visual element such as a piece of sculpture, a specimen tree, or an attractive pot with plants. A roomy landing also allows guests to comfortably enter your home.

Consider how the materials and patterns used in your walkways relate to the rest of the garden. For example, precast odd-shaped pavers leading up to a stately home may look out of place, but in a less-formal setting, the same treatment could be charming.

GARDEN PATHS

Perhaps the most important function of a garden path is to show off the landscape. In most cases, a person walking down a meandering path moves slowy to enjoy the experience. The pathway offers a wonderful opportunity to showcase your favorite view, a plant, a fountain, or a comfortable seating area.

Garden paths may be more narrow than front walks. If the path does not need to accommodate a lot of traffic, a two- to three-foot width is suitable for one person to stroll comfortably along.

Materials suitable for garden paths are more varied than those for front walks. Here, you do not necessarily have to be able to accommodate dress shoes, therefore mulches and crushed gravel can be used. Stone, brick, and precast pavers are also popular choices.

A ground cover planted around the stepping stones softens the look of this path and blends it into the surrounding landscape. Low-growing herbs are a wonderful choice for planting in a path, releasing their fragrance when you step on them.

STEPS

In most of the South, it is not uncommon to have grade changes in the landscape. And in some cases, if you have a relatively flat piece of land, you may even want to create an elevation change, such as a sunken garden or raised terrace, just to spice up the garden. Steps are commonly used to accommodate these grade changes.

Having the proper relationship between the treads (the part you step on) and the risers (the difference in elevation from one step to the next) will help ensure that your steps are both safe and comfortable. Generally speaking, the shorter the riser the longer the tread, but treads less than eleven inches or risers less than four inches or greater than seven inches are not recommended.

Keep in mind that all steps in a series should be the same size. Each tread should be the same depth and each rise the same height. Avoid having one step by itself; it will be difficult to see and may cause people to trip. If the steps will be used at night, you will need to be sure they are lit properly.

Broad flagstone steps virtually terrace this slope, making the ascent comfortable and gradual. Railroad ties serve as risers; their color is a pleasing accent and also helps visitors see the changes in level more clearly.

Step Dimensions

It is commonly accepted that two risers plus a tread should equal twenty-six inches (2R + T=26). This will help you figure out how many steps you need and what dimensions they should have.

For example, if you have twenty-two inches of elevation change (known as the total rise), find a whole number which, if divided into the total rise, yields a number between four and seven. For instance, a total rise of twenty-two inches divided by four is five-and-one-half. Therefore, you could build four steps that rise five-and-one-half inches each. Using the formula given above, you can determine that the treads need to be fifteen inches deep (2 x 5½ + 15 = 26).

All steps in a series should be the same size, but inserting a broader tread at the fifth step from the bottom breaks up this flight of stone stairs so that the climb seems less daunting.

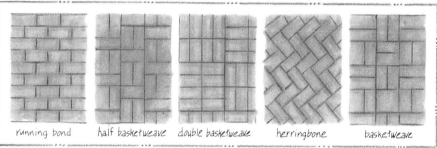

running bond   half basketweave   double basketweave   herringbone   basketweave

PAVING

Dozens of different materials are available for surfacing your driveways, walkways, and pathways. For all paving materials, consider their appearance, the function they will serve, and their durability. In many cases, the same materials suitable for paving drives and walks are ideally suited for terraces and courtyards as well. In fact, repeating a paving material in different areas is an excellent way to help unify the garden.

There are many different installation techniques for paving materials, but for our purposes we will consider two: setting materials in mortar or otherwise fixing them in place, and positioning materials without mortar.

Mortared sections of slate pavers rest in a bed of pea gravel, above right. A grid of exposed aggregate and smooth concrete (right) makes this parking area an attractive design element.

FIXED MATERIALS

POURING IN PLACE

Concrete and asphalt are the most common types of pavement which are poured in place. Other materials which are poured in place include tabby and exposed aggregate paving.

Concrete is the most common paving material in the landscape. It is durable, versatile, relatively inexpensive, easy to work with, and can be finished in many different ways.

Concrete is composed of portland cement, water, and some sort of aggregate such as sand or gravel. When the cement and water are mixed, they fill the voids between the aggregate and form a solid mass. After an initial setting period of about ten hours, concrete continues to set for about twenty-eight days before it is "cured."

Because it can be poured and shaped into almost any form, concrete is the most versatile of paving materials. Concrete used in the landscape is often reinforced with steel to resist changes in temperatures and shrinking.

Concrete is popular for drives, parking areas, walks, and terraces. If you think that concrete is boring and plain, consider the advances in staining and setting patterns in concrete. Many colors of stain can be added to the concrete as it is mixed. The finished result can range from gray to green to pink to black. There are also stains that can be added after the concrete is in place, but they do not last as long as those mixed in at the start.

Putting a finish or pattern on the concrete is another way to enhance its appearance. One simple

As the name implies, fixed materials are more permanent. There are two commonly used techniques for fixing materials: pouring in place and setting in mortar.

technique is called a broom finish. This can be accomplished by lightly brushing a straw broom over the surface of a wet slab of concrete. The straw will rough the surface and give it a texture that is slip-resistant and more visually appealing.

Stamping concrete involves selecting from a wide range of metal stamps that can be pressed into the concrete to give the appearance of individual pavers. When used in conjunction with a stain, this technique can easily give the appearance of brick, cobblestone, or slate.

Tabby is a material indigenous to coastal areas and is a mix of limestone, shell, and sand. It sets in a concrete-like appearance with a pocked surface of exposed bits of shell.

Exposed aggregate paving is created by adding small, washed stones to a standard concrete mix. After the concrete is poured, a thin layer is washed off with a hose to expose the stones for a textured surface. Another method is to epoxy aggregate to the surface. One drawback to this type of paving is that it can be slippery when wet, since a smaller aggregate is ordinarily used.

Concrete paving requires a base and a form. The base can be as simple as a layer of gravel and the form can be made of two-by-fours nailed into the desired shape. For more critical features such as terraces and drives, building a base and form is more involved, so you may want to consult a professional designer or contractor.

A concrete surface looks like slate when you paint it with flat, exterior acrylic latex house paint in five shades of gray. The original concrete shows through to simulate mortar.

Asphalt is a common material for driveways and parking areas. It is not recommended for walks or terraces around homes because it can be spongy and gives off fumes when heated by the sun.

The popularity of asphalt comes from its ease of placement and flexibility. When used properly, asphalt can withstand extremes of weather and the prying roots of trees better than concrete. It is also less expensive than concrete, however, it will fall into disrepair more rapidly.

SETTING IN MORTAR

This category of paving includes brick, stone, slate, granite, precast pavers, tile, and anything else you set in mortar. A big advantage to using this type of paving is that you can develop an infinite number of patterns since each piece of paving is placed individually. The biggest drawback to this type of paving is the cost that results from the amount of labor involved.

Regardless of the material you use, the procedure for paving is basically the same. The area to be paved is excavated, a frame is built to define the edges, then a base layer of gravel and/or sand is added. On top of the base, a thin layer of mortar or concrete is applied and then the paving material is set on top of that. Additional mortar is added between the joints to make it water tight and to prevent slippage.

If you have never shopped for paving materials before, you might be surprised at the wide selection. There are dozens of styles of brick available. The same can be said for stone and precast pavers. While it may take longer to make the right choice, the availability of so many materials ensures finding the perfect one for your garden.

You may want to consider mixing materials. This is particularly helpful if the material best suited for one area is different from paving used elsewhere in the garden. For example, you might have a concrete driveway but want a brick walk. Using brick headers or edging to frame a concrete walk is a way to unite these materials.

PAVING WITHOUT MORTAR

There are many advantages to using paving material that is not set in mortar. It involves less expertise, so it is usually less expensive. You can remove it or change it if you need to, and you do not have to sacrifice anything in appearance. It also allows water to drain easily.

The materials that lend themselves to this type of paving are those with relatively smooth and even edges. This allows the different pieces to fit together snugly for a more stable surface. Bricks, flat stones, and precast pavers are good examples.

Installing this type of paving is a little less complicated than setting paving in mortar. All you need is a frame (usually made of wood and left in place) that has taken into account the dimensions of the pavers. You want the pavers to fit tightly in order to minimize shifting. Inside the frame, a layer of sand or fine gravel is added and then leveled. On top of the sand, the pavers are set in place and then more sand is swept in-between the units for a tight fit.

One popular and versatile material becoming more readily available is the precast interlocking paver. It does not require any mortar to hold it in place but is exceptionally stable due to the interlocking design. These pavers fit together much like the pieces of a puzzle. A variety of shapes and finishes are available.

Another approach to creating walks and drives without mortar is to use loose materials such as pea gravel, crushed granite, or mulch. One big advantage to this type of material is that you do not have to worry about drainage because water percolates through. On the other hand, car tires push the material into rows and you may observe some washing away of the material during heavy rains. To prevent washing, you will need an edging high enough to keep the material in bounds. Inevitably you will need to add more of the material over time as it settles or is knocked or washed out of bounds.

While loose materials are appealing due to their relatively low cost and ease of installation, they do have limitations. For instance, walking on gravel while wearing high heels is challenging, as is rolling a garden cart or wheelbarrow. Usually these materials are best suited for informal garden paths, drives, or parking areas. Keep in mind that if the material is white or has a reflective quality, it can be difficult to blend into the landscape.

MIXING PLANTS AND PAVERS

Paver after paver after paver can be pretty dull, but a walkway or terrace that contrasts living plants against a hard surface can be very exciting. This simple concept offers an endless combination of paving materials and ground covers. You can find a look to suit any garden.

For example, a rectangular lawn in a formal garden can be made more durable, while retaining its formal look, by partially filling it with brick paving pads to create a terrace effect. On the other hand, a large entry court built with precast concrete pavers can be made more inviting by using plants instead of mortar between the pavers.

Almost any type of paving can be used effectively with plants.

However, individual pavers such as precast concrete, exposed aggregate, or stones lend themselves to this better because they can be dry laid.

Plants help soften the hard lines and edges of brick, concrete, and stone. This can subdue the impact a paved area has on the landscape. Planting affects scale, too. A band of dwarf mondo grass crossing a long brick walk at regular intervals makes the walk appear shorter, visually bringing it down to a more intimate scale.

Plants can give a walkway a pleasing patina. It takes mortar years to weather, while mondo grass, carpet bugleweed, and other ground covers will usually fill in over one or two growing seasons.

When selecting plants, there are several considerations. First, use a plant that blends with the overall garden design. If you want an unobtrusive stone walkway through a lawn, you will get better results by allowing grass to grow between the pavers than by adding a ground cover. You may want to use a path as an opportunity to repeat a ground cover that is being used elsewhere in the garden. This will help to unify the design. Whatever you choose, be sure it can withstand at least moderate foot traffic. Most lawns, mondo grass, low-growing sedums, and carpet bugleweed are good examples of durable plants. A low growth habit is another necessary trait. Plants that reach no more than four inches in height are best.

Always select plants well suited to the amount of sun they will receive. Low-growing herbs such as creeping thyme, Corsican mint, and chamomile all need a sunny location.

Plants give a pathway instant character. Blue phlox spills over the edges of cobblestone pads (left); dwarf mondo grass makes a tidy edging for the stepping stones (above) and reproduces on a smaller scale the texture of the liriope lining the walk.

Chapter Four

Gates, Walls, And Fences

*G*ates, walls, and fences mark the garden's border, ensure privacy, and define the spaces within. These features also provide security and restrict and direct how people and pets move through the garden. But their most valuable contribution may be that little element of intrigue and romance they so effortlessly introduce into the garden.

GATES

At first glance, a garden gate seems a simple thing—an entry to the garden. A closer look reveals that a well-designed and thoughtfully placed gate can do much more than provide access.

A garden gate sets a mood and adds visual interest. Opening a gate gives a moment to pause and appreciate the subtle colors and sweet fragrances of nearby blossoms. An open-style gate piques curiosity by allowing a glimpse of what lies ahead. A gate tucked into an out-of-the-way corner seems mysterious. A solid gate enhances a garden feature suddenly revealed when the gate is opened.

A gate can be a focal point. If a bright white gate leads through an evergreen hedge, the gate will stand out because it contrasts so sharply with its background. Set at one end of a garden, such a gate will draw your eye across the entire length of the space. If the gate can be opened to frame a vista, then the surrounding landscape becomes a part of the garden design as well.

The character of the space beyond can be reflected in a gate's design. For example, a low gate seems friendly and bids welcome. You might choose a gate less than waist high to lead visitors into an entry garden at the front door. On the other hand, a gate several feet tall may be more appropriate in your backyard or near the pool to indicate that the area is private and just for invited guests.

Architectural harmony is one of the main considerations when planning your gate's style. Often, details which are used elsewhere in the garden can be repeated in the gate design to create a sense of repetition or unity. If the doors that lead to your garden from inside the house feature an unusual molding, you might use that same molding on the gate. Or the pattern in a porch rail could be worked into the gate's design.

Whatever the style, be aware that quality building materials and hardware are essential. Use pressure-treated or other rot-resistant lumber for wooden gates, and select hinges and fasteners that will not rust or stain. If the gate is meant to simply admit people, then a three-foot width is sufficient. However, if the gate is the only access to an area, it should be wide enough to accommodate a garden cart or any other equipment you may need inside.

Whether fanciful or sophisticated, a well-designed gate can communicate something of the garden's personality—and yours.

WALLS

Wall designs can vary greatly. They can be straight, angled, or serpentine. They can be solid or have an open design to allow air to circulate. Regardless of the style you choose, be sure the materials blend with the house and other elements of the garden. Keep in mind that walls painted with dark colors will tend to recede, bright colors will stand out. Climbing plants or a planting in front of the wall will help soften a broad expanse of masonry.

A retaining wall serves a functional purpose. This type of wall holds back soil that results from changing the slope of the land. A retaining wall is used most frequently when terracing a site, which is an effective way to create spaces in the garden and is often the only way to have a level area.

The style of a retaining wall is often governed by structural concerns, yet the finished wall can be an attractive garden accent. Stuccoed or painted concrete block, dry-stacked stone, stone set in mortar, and landscape timbers are materials commonly used in retaining walls.

Gates that open like French doors in a brick wall (above) convey the feeling of entering an outdoor room. Repeating the crossed-bar motif of the gate along the top of the wall ties the two together visually. A free-standing gate (right) linking two planting beds is as much a focal point as a functional divider.

Filling the arched openings of this wall with lattice panels preserves privacy without blocking air circulation. Bougainvillea and purple heart soften the lines of the wall. Their colors accent the pale pink of the stucco.

A retaining wall of stacked stone makes a handsome backdrop for hosta.

On steeply sloping sites, retaining walls allow you to carve out level areas for planting. Pressure-treated timbers are a relatively inexpensive alternative to stone or concrete.

Openings pierce the brick wall (top) to let breezes flow through, a critical consideration in humid areas. (Poor air circulation and high humidity not only make the garden an uncomfortable place to be but also contribute to problems with mold and rot on plants.) Retaining walls of stone set in mortar define and contain the sloping front yard (above).

HEDGES

Formal hedges require regular shaping to maintain the desired appearance.

Hedges can be used to form living garden walls. They can do almost anything a fence or wall can, but a row of trees or shrubs can also offer seasonal color, changeable form, and a softer look than masonry or wood.

One of the most common uses of a hedge is as a screen. A dense row of evergreen trees or large shrubs, such as hemlock or waxleaf privet, can easily block an unsightly view. For a smaller hedge, use medium-size shrubs such as glossy abelia, dwarf Burford holly, or common boxwood.

Hedges provide an attractive means of wind control. A strategically placed row of Leyland cypress or elaeagnus can block winter winds (usually out of the northwest) and significantly reduce heating costs. For wind control, plant trees and shrubs close together and near the house (within twenty to thirty feet); otherwise, the wind will go over the tops of the plants and down again to hit the house.

Hedges may help control traffic through the garden. Thorny shrubs, including selections of holly and wintergreen barberry, make an attractive and functional barrier. You can divert traffic in a more subtle way by using a low-growing hedge of edging boxwood or dwarf yaupon.

Parterres and mazes are two kinds of hedges used purely for aesthetics. These fanciful and high-maintenance plantings are found most commonly in formal gardens, such as those in Colonial Williamsburg.

CULTURAL CONSIDERATIONS

When you plan your hedge, consider the texture, color, and form of the plants you want to use. A row of free-form forsythia in bloom, the red berries of holly in winter, and the fine texture of boxwood offer a look no wooden fence or brick wall can match.

Whichever plant you choose, be sure that it is a selection that grows well in your climate. Familiarize yourself with the plant's fruiting and flowering habits to make sure it blends into your overall color scheme.

Hedges enclose space and block strong winds as effectively as masonry or wood. You have to wait longer to enjoy their benefits, but once mature, hedges provide natural form and the potential for seasonal color.

Knowing a plant's mature size and growth rate will enable you to space it properly. Spacing will vary depending on the plants you use and what you are trying to accomplish with them. As a general rule for a hedge used as a screen, select plants that will grow at least four feet thick. For a low border that controls where people walk or accents a drive, approximately two feet should be wide enough.

Parterres like those at Cedar Lane Farms rely on low hedges to outline beds in geometric shapes.

MASSING SHRUBS

Massing shrubs can serve many of the same functions as a hedge, fence, or wall. When used to surround a terrace, this technique is an effective way to set the area apart from the rest of the garden. If the plants you select bloom, the terrace can seem at times to float within a cloud of color. This same technique can be used to define areas of the garden, direct views, and provide privacy. A mass of shrubs differs in some ways from a hedge. While a hedge is a group of plants that forms a row, a mass has greater depth, can undulate, and is less formal in appearance.

When massing shrubs, the most critical decision is the choice of plants. In effect, they become your building materials. You need to be aware of the mature size of the plant (both height and width), any blooming or fruiting characteristics it may possess, and how much maintenance it will require. As you select shrubs, limit the number of species in any given mass. A sweep of one species often creates a more dramatic visual impact than a mixed planting.

If using more than one type of plant in a grouping, it is important to consider how the different plants relate to each other aesthetically and horticulturally. Be careful to avoid mixing plants with widely varying light, water, and fertilizer requirements.

One of the beauties of a mass of shrubs is that it is designed to grow together, all but eliminating the need to prune. As a general rule, plant larger shrubs at the rear or center of the bed with smaller shrubs in front or toward the end of the bed. As you select

your plants, explore the use of plant texture to add interest to the garden.

Spacing is critical in a shrub mass. Keep in mind the growth habits of the plants and allow enough space for the plants to reach their mature size. The plants should be close enough to each other to form a solid surface without being crowded. You will have to be patient when planting young shrubs, or for a more immediate effect, you may decide to plant larger specimens.

For several weeks each spring, this mass of azaleas dazzles the eye with color. The rest of the year, it is a low, living wall of green that subtly divides the space.

FENCES

Iron and wood are the most common materials used for building fences, but there is an endless array of styles. The choice of materials and the design of the fence should be compatible with the house and any other structures within the garden. For example, a split-rail fence is incongruous with a formal home. Likewise, a picket fence is typically not a good match for a contemporary home.

A security fence should have a minimum height of eight feet. Since security fences do not necessarily have to screen a view, there is an infinite choice. For a privacy fence, you will need a height of at least six feet. Before you finalize your design, find out about any building restrictions that may limit height.

Often a fence is needed to keep children and pets where you want them or away from where you do not want them. This type of fence does not need to be as tall as a security or privacy fence.

Picket fences serve this purpose well and are popular for good reason. They are relatively easy and inexpensive to build, and they are easy to personalize. Simply changing the pattern of the slats or adding finials (post caps) can give you a unique look.

Many times a fence is desired simply to define part of the garden, whether it is an entryway, flower garden, terrace, or the entire border of the property. Fences of this type are usually about three feet high. A picket fence works well for this use, too.

Chainlink is one of the most widely used types of fences, largely because it is widely available and less expensive than many alternative ways of securing property. For a more attractive appearance, chainlink can be painted a dark color to help it fade into the background. Choose a paint that is formulated for exterior, metal surfaces, and be sure to use a flat paint, not a semi-gloss or glossy one. Another idea is to screen the fence with plants or a vine.

Planted with vines tumbling over the top, a white picket fence suggests both a friendly feeling and a cozy sense of home. No wonder this type of fence is popular—it is relatively easy and inexpensive to build, it looks neat and tidy, and it is just the right height for neighborly conversations.

Split-rail fences are romantic and rustic, conjuring images of the countryside. Although they once kept horses and cows from wandering off, they are now purely decorative.

A solid wooden fence at least six feet tall provides privacy and some security. Training pyracantha to follow the vertical and horizontal supports helps temper the rigid lines and makes the fence a more interesting feature in the garden.

The enclosure around a pool need not be taller than a picket fence to keep children where you want them or away from where you don't.

This Chinese Chippendale design allows light and air to reach the shrubs on the other side. Painting both the wood and its masonry base white yields a formal look.

Iron bars and concrete pillars constitute one of the sturdiest, longest-lasting fences you can build. A graceful curve in this one mitigates the severity of the design and serves to frame the house.

Openwork panels add a light, decorative accent to walls of solid wood linked by brick piers.

EDGING

The idea of edging a garden has been around a long time, and the benefits are numerous. Besides bordering flowerbeds and accenting lines of the landscape, edging helps simplify garden maintenance. While it keeps plants and mulch in their place, it can also double as a mowing strip, eliminating the need for string trimming the border of a lawn.

Steel, wood, plastic, stone, and brick are all suitable materials for edging. The material you select should serve whatever needs you have and fit in with the rest of the building materials as well. For example, a low stone edging may be your first choice, but if the edging needs to hold back a bed of mulch, you may want to use a taller, brick edging.

Brick is a particularly appealing material for edging. There are many different styles from which to choose, and all offer a distinctive look. A brick edging is often more formal in appearance than stone or wood. Brick's permanent surface will resist the wear of a string trimmer better than wood or plastic.

Because brick is used for many homes, terraces, and walls, repeating it as an edging in the garden is a good way to unify these different components. You can also use it to unify different paving materials. For example, a brick-edged concrete walk that

Brick edging (above) offers a formal look and can double as a mowing strip. Dry-laid gray stone (right) makes a beautiful foil for most flower colors.

To establish the line for a curving border, use a garden hose to lay out the design. Mark the line with a spade or with spray paint.

meets a brick-lined asphalt drive results in a smooth transition.

Before you start an edging project, consider both the material and the design best suited to your situation. Your choices range from a simple row of bricks laid end to end, to elaborate patterns that can double as a pathway. With so many choices, it is best to shop around for ideas. Look at a neighbor's garden, books, or consult with a landscape architect for ideas and suggestions.

Putting Brick Edging Into Place

Whether your edging has a straight or curved pattern will depend on personal taste as well as the design of the garden.

Straight lines can be established easily by driving two stakes in the ground and running a string between them. Put the stakes a bit beyond the point where the edging will end so they will not be in the way as you lay the brick.

For a *curving line*, try using a garden hose to lay out the design. Mark along the hose using a spade, pour sand along it, or use spray paint to mark the line.

In most cases, setting the material in a bed of sand—called dry laid—will be sufficient to keep it in place. Over a period of time, sand settles around the bricks making them sturdy. However, not every edging style lends itself to this technique. Setting the edging in mortar will make it especially durable. Wood, steel, and plastic edging will need to be staked into place.

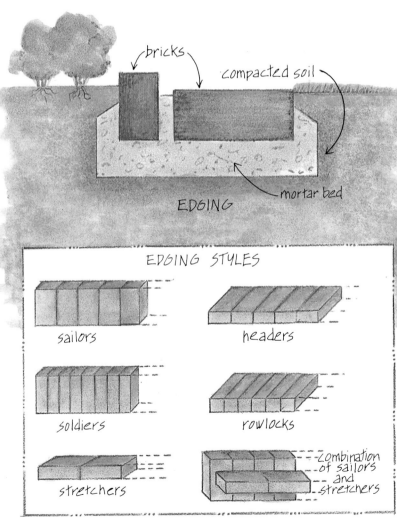

bricks

compacted soil

mortar bed

EDGING

EDGING STYLES

sailors

headers

soldiers

rowlocks

stretchers

combination of sailors and stretchers

Chapter Five

SIDEYARDS,
COURTYARDS,
And
GETAWAYS

The area alongside your house may have untapped potential. A paved walk, a bench, planting beds, and begonia-filled planters turn this sideyard into an intimate retreat. The view from inside the house is now more attractive too.

One of the greatest pleasures of a garden is relaxing in a private getaway spot as you enjoy the sights, sounds, and smells that surround you. This feeling of intimacy with the garden depends largely on creating a space that enhances the experience.

A sideyard, courtyard, or secluded garden area is the perfect setting for an intimate garden space. With a little design ingenuity, you can have a garden getaway that will give you a pleasant reward every day you spend in the garden.

SIDEYARDS

The sideyard is often ignored while the front and back receive all of our time and attention. After all, who among us does not enter that friendly competition for the greenest front lawn in the neighborhood? We work hard to make our backyards pleasant as well, because we spend so much of our leisure time there. But too often the sideyard sits forlornly between the two, neglected and unsightly.

As gardens become smaller, however, the status of sideyards rises. The increased attention devoted to sideyards is simply the result of limited space. Land costs are high, so lots are small, but the houses are as big as ever. That leaves less and less usable area outdoors. Often, much of the front yard is taken up by off-street parking, and the backyard may be taken up by a pool or garage. In such cases, the sideyard becomes extremely valuable simply because it is the only space available.

Some of the most appealing sideyards are composed of a simple walkway leading from the front yard to the back, with well-designed planting areas on either side. This path can become the major entrance to the backyard and serves to whet a visitor's appetite for what lies ahead. Along the walk, consider planting a variety of evergreens, flowering shrubs, bulbs, annuals, perennials, and ferns to offer colors and textures that change with every season.

Because sideyards are usually narrow, next-door neighbors are often quite close by, so screening unattractive views and the need for privacy become major design factors. If the neighbor's house is the first thing you see when you walk outside, you may want to direct the eye away from that view to a focal point in your own garden, such as a piece of sculpture or a specimen plant. To obscure a neighbor's second-story view into your garden, consider adding an arbor over part of the space to help increase the sense of privacy.

Sideyards are the connecting link between the garden spaces in front of and behind your house. They can provide visual links to what lies ahead.

An appealing sideyard can be as simple as an attractive path bordered by well-chosen plantings.

A courtyard should be a jewel box, an open-air room outfitted with meticulous attention to detail.

Building courtyard walls and floor from brick that matches the house (previous page and above) makes the outdoor room appear to be an extension of the architecture. Small trees screen the gray brick wall (previous page) and keep the space from feeling boxy. Above, river birch and tea olive preserve privacy by blocking the view into the courtyard from neighboring houses.

COURTYARDS

Courtyards, by definition, are enclosed on the sides and left open to the sky overhead. This design accounts for their vast appeal. They offer privacy, yet they are open to the fresh air and sunlight. They are, in the truest sense, outdoor rooms.

In some cases, a courtyard is formed when a long, narrow house goes all the way to the back property line. That leaves a long, narrow space along one side, with rooms looking out in that direction. Often the best solution to this situation is to enclose the garden space with a high wall and make it an outdoor extension of the house.

Whether you have a courtyard adjacent to one room or a larger courtyard accessed by several rooms, consider the relationship between what is happening inside the house and the courtyard itself. Often this relationship will determine the design and use of the courtyard. For example, if it adjoins the dining room, a logical use for the courtyard would be an outdoor dining area. If it adjoins a study or living room, you may want to expand your living area to the outdoors.

Because courtyards are usually small, attention to detail is very important. All elements in a courtyard are observed at close range, so flaws and imperfections are going to be more noticeable. If you include high-maintenance elements in your courtyard, neglect will be more evident, but you can solve the problem ahead of time through proper design.

Keeping this Florida courtyard tidy is easy with low-maintenance plantings. Tropical plants provide structure (and the palms merge with those outdoors). Impatiens supply mounds of color.

This outdoor room offers views to enjoy from above as well as space for entertaining in the courtyard itself. When choosing plants, consider their ultimate dimensions and maintenance requirements as well as their resistance to pests and diseases.

Selecting plants that grow slowly is one simple way of keeping a courtyard looking good with a minimum of maintenance. Avoiding trees that shed catkins or leaves is another. When selecting plants for a courtyard, consider their ultimate size and find out whether or not they are prone to diseases and pests. Wind circulation is hindered in an enclosed space, so the incidence of pest problems is often higher.

As you design a courtyard, approach it as you would a room inside the house. Once the purpose has been determined, map out where to put the "furniture." Some of the furniture may literally be furniture, but plants, fountains, and sculpture define and accent space as well. The use of container plants becomes especially important in a courtyard.

A courtyard off the dining room (above) offers a place to enjoy meals outdoors. These spaces are also ideal for displaying sculpture or special garden ornaments that can be enjoyed at close range (right).

GETAWAYS

Civilization may have moved us out of the woods and into the house, but the lure of nature lingers. Many of us still want a place away from the telephone and television, a quiet place to relax and enjoy being out-of-doors.

Your private spot can be as simple as a bench set off from a path or tucked away in a corner. It might be as elaborate as an arbor situated in the most isolated part of your property. Its location will be determined in part by the size and shape of the garden and by what is going on immediately around it. Regardless of the size or location, success depends heavily on several design factors: orientation, enclosure, and enrichment.

In many cases, the most important feature of a getaway is its orientation, or the direction it faces, since what you see from within a secluded area sets the mood. And remember, the eye can be easily fooled. Just as objects can be made to appear larger or smaller than they really are, the illusion of isolation can be accomplished through design.

If you are looking for a spot to get away in your garden, take a walk around and simply observe. Take note of where you have good or bad views. This will help you decide whether to face into or out of the garden. Having the getaway face a wooded or natural area can be very effective.

All the ingredients for a secluded retreat are here: a place to sit, the sheltering canopy of trees, and a view framed by a break in the garden wall.

A garden getaway invites you to immerse yourself in the sights, sounds, and scents of your own private Eden.

Another way for a garden getaway to be effective is enclosure. You can provide enclosure many ways—a dense hedge of evergreen trees or shrubs, a brick wall, or a wooden fence are just a few examples. The materials used will vary, but as a general rule, plants have the bonus of visually defining an area while creating the feeling of being close to nature.

An important element of enclosure is what is overhead. Whether it is the spreading branches of a shade tree or a vine-covered arbor, most getaways have some sort of canopy. Having something limiting your view tends to focus attention on the immediate surroundings.

You can also gain a feeling of being away from it all through changes in level. If you have a small yard, you will probably want to create a feeling of distance or destination. Steps, terraces, and other level changes are good ways to do this. For a hilly terrain, consider high or low spots for a greater sense of separation.

Rich detailing will make a big difference in your getaway. Enrich this area with the sights, sounds, and smells you enjoy. These secluded areas are ideal for close-up views of plants or sculpture. You may want a bed of favorite annuals nearby so you can watch their daily progress, or maybe a planting of fragrant herbs or flowers. If you like birds, include a feeder, birdbath, or other lures. Consider adding speakers so you can listen to music.

An arbor offers the sense of enclosure that a getaway requires. It is also a major garden structure and can serve as a focal point to anchor your landscape design.

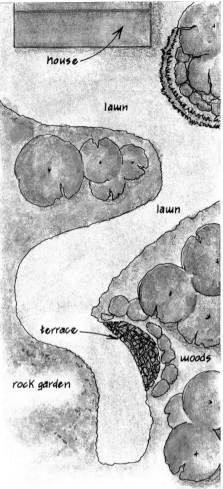

Carve an oasis of tranquility into a wooded setting simply by creating a free-standing terrace of stones. The crescent-shaped spot (left) works around existing trees and overlooks the rock garden.

The arbor (left) gains a sense of destination by being sited at the end of a series of steps and terraces (see drawing below).

A hammock represents the ultimate invitation to get away from it all. Ringed by trees and shrubs, the island of lawn (top) is reached by a narrow path that enhances its feeling of remoteness (see drawing above).

PLANTING IN SMALL SPACES

In addition to cultural considerations, color and fragrance are important. If there is a lot of brickwork, for instance, try using evergreens to make the space feel softer, then add color in pots, since brightly colored blooms may conflict with the red of the brick.

Fragrance is a frequently overlooked aspect of the plant palette. Smell is one of the most evocative of all the senses, and the opportunity to capture a scent in an enclosed space is greater than in any other part of the garden. Keep this in mind as you choose your plants and consider adding a gardenia, daphne, tea olive, or other fragrant plants to your garden.

CONTAINER PLANTS

One of the chief advantages of plants in containers is their flexibility. If you get tired of where they are, you can simply rearrange them. This not only allows you to try different locations but also enables you to move plants to a sheltered location during winter months.

Often, using containers is the only way to introduce plants into an area that would otherwise be void of them. Plants in containers can create a nice transition between the house and garden.

A variety of containers work together here to put color at different heights.

Make the most of small, enclosed spaces by choosing plants with fragrance. The evanescent pleasure of scented plants is one of the best reasons to have containers in areas you pass through often.

If you envision a deck, terrace, or courtyard as an outdoor room, then consider how container plants can help structure the walls of that room or even divide one large area into smaller ones. You can also use plants to frame pleasant views.

In addition to defining new spaces, container plants can be used to highlight exisiting architecture. For example, if you have symmetrical architecture, you can emphasize that symmetry with a few strategically placed container plants.

Three large pots of Lily-of-the-Nile placed beside the door can be enjoyed from indoors or outside.

CHOOSING PLANTS AND CONTAINERS

Urns, baskets, barrels, plastic or clay pots—the variety of plant containers is endless. However, your primary considerations when choosing containers should be that they are attractive and provide a healthy growing environment, which means space for roots, proper aeration of soil, and good drainage.

The objective is to make the right choice for your region, setting, and design objectives. Because you are usually working with a limited space, each plant and container needs to be selected carefully for its interest and its function. For example, if you want to screen an area, you need to use a plant and container large enough to do that. For accents and spots of color, use smaller containers.

If gardeners had to choose only one type of pot, many would opt for clay. Clay pots are easy to find, serviceable, inexpensive, and blend well with most outdoor settings. Plants, too, prefer clay, because this porous material permits the passage of air so that roots can breathe. Though some distinctive containers and plants can become permanent architectural features in a garden, in colder areas of the South where freezing weather may crack porous clay, terra-cotta, and earthenware, it is best to plant for a seasonal display, then move planters into a basement or garage for the winter.

Wooden planters tolerate cold weather but will eventually rot. One way to extend the life of a wooden container is to apply a sealant to its interior and exterior. Another way is to insert a plastic

In most cases, outdoor containers like these geranium-filled pots should be large to be in scale with the outdoor setting.

If you choose an upright plant for a container (left and above), add a cascading one at its base to trail or reach over the edge of the pot. This yields visual balance and links the planting to the ground.

pot or metal liner into the planter so that soil does not come in contact with the wood. Elevating the planter slightly with small blocks will create an air space beneath it and help delay rotting. You may want to consider a planter made of teak, cypress, redwood, or other woods that resist rot.

Plastic containers are readily available and are the least expensive of all varieties. Several manufacturers make plastic containers that closely resemble wood, terracotta, or other materials, and some of these are actually growing systems that feature built-in reservoirs for water.

Naturally, you want the container to suit the cultural needs of the plant, but it should also blend aesthetically. If you have an especially elegant or detailed container, you should use it where it will be appreciated. Then, in areas where details are less important,

use simple containers. To avoid cluttering an area, it is best to limit the number of different styles of containers you use.

Pay particular attention to the scale of both the plant and the container. Consider how they relate to each other and how the combined plant and container relate to the house and setting. Be careful not to put small household pots on a terrace because they are usually way out of scale. In most cases, you do not want to use outdoor containers smaller than ten inches wide. This takes into consideration how the size of the pot fits the setting as well as the extra maintenance required for small containers. The container size also depends on the size of the space and the plants you plan to use. Plan on using smaller containers as embellishment to a design structured by a few large plants in large containers.

No matter which containers you choose, keep them as clean and attractive as the plants growing in them. Wooden pots may mildew during the summer, and green algae may stain those made from concrete or clay. Scrubbing with a stiff brush dipped in a solution of one part bleach and nine parts water will solve both problems.

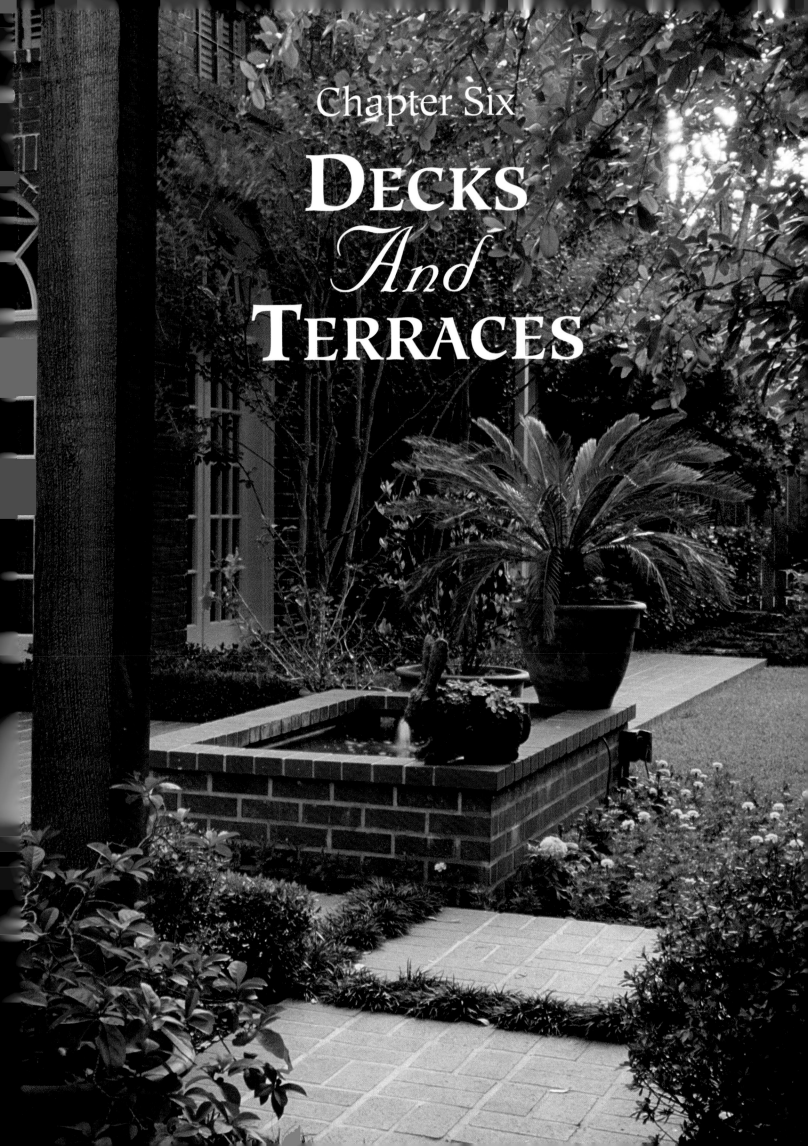

Chapter Six

DECKS
And
TERRACES

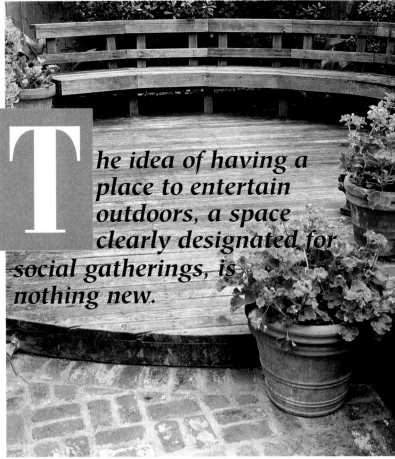

The idea of having a place to entertain outdoors, a space clearly designated for social gatherings, is nothing new.

The villas of northern Italy and the estates of France show us that terraces have been integral parts of garden design for centuries. And going back even further in time, Oriental designs have made use of decks for thousands of years. Of course, terraces and decks are not just for entertaining. They provide a perfect place to sit, relax, and enjoy your garden.

At first glance, decks and terraces may seem worlds apart. One is set above the ground and the other rests firmly on the soil. One is made of wood and the other is made of masonry. But they have more similarities than differences when it comes to function. Both provide a level place to set up tables and chairs for entertaining, typically they are adjacent to the house and become an extension of it, and both can offer commanding views of the garden.

Terraces (left) are made of brick, concrete, or stone and usually rest directly on the ground. Decks (above) are built from wood and are therefore raised above the ground anywhere from a few inches to many feet.

DECKS

The very word evokes images of breezy afternoons sitting high above the garden with tree limbs swaying at eye level. A deck does a lot to expand your living area. It provides an outdoor space for cookouts and for kids to play and is especially useful for entertaining.

In many cases, building a deck is a project you can do yourself, making it even more affordable. In general, the more angular and intricate the design, the harder a deck is to build. Unless you have had a good bit of carpentry experience, you may find it easier to stay with straight edges and square corners for your design. Or design the deck of your dreams and have the work done.

There are many types of decks. You can have a deck on top of your garage, or you can use decking to cover up an unsightly concrete pad that was meant to be a terrace. A deck can be used to provide a level area on a steep lot, or you can have a free-standing deck in a remote part of the garden.

Location is determined largely by how you intend to use the deck. If you want it to be an extension of the family or living rooms, the spot will be decided for you. But there is no need to limit yourself to any one area.

Whether you want a deck for sunbathing or prefer a shady place to sit, pay attention to sun patterns when choosing a location. Areas receiving

A deck can expand your living space enormously. In these examples (above and right), decks provide level areas on sloping lots.

*Whether a deck is large or small,
comfortable seating and leafy plants will
make it more inviting.*

The decks (above and right) were designed to unify different areas and to accommodate existing plantings. The railing (above) doubles as extra seating. Raised planting areas (right) provide space for flowers.

sunlight in the winter may be shady in spring and summer when leaves come out on deciduous trees. Also be aware of prevailing winds, exceptional views, and any water that drips from rooflines or trees.

Once you have the location and basic size, you need a shape that not only suits your needs but blends with the rest of the house and garden. For example, a perfectly square deck built onto the back of a long, low house may fulfill your needs but will look out of place. A rectangular one might look better and still have the same square footage. Decks can also be used to unite irregular spaces created by the house. For large decks, you may want to alternate the floor level for visual interest.

As you design your deck, ask friends and neighbors who have decks for suggestions and recommendations. Visit lumber yards and home centers to look at plans, or look through books and magazines for ideas. You may want to consult with a landscape architect at this time for ideas on customizing a deck for your house and garden.

Railing and other details offer an opportunity to be truly creative. Deck railing can be as elaborate as a custom-designed Chippendale pattern or as simple as a row of slats. The style should reflect the detailing of the house or nearby structures. Be sure to check local ordinances about railings. The height of the deck usually determines whether or not you will need to add a railing.

A seat/railing combination is a practical approach to deck railing. This design provides the safety of a railing while offering a place to sit as well. You may even design the seat with storage underneath, which is perfect for storing cushions and other outdoor gear.

OUTDOOR BUILDING MATERIALS

The lasting success of a deck or any outdoor project built of wood depends largely on the materials used for construction. That includes lumber as well as hardware.

Redwood, cedar, and cypress are all good choices. Though more expensive than other types of lumber, you may want to consider them for their refined appearance. While these types of wood are naturally resistant to decay, finishing them with water repellents and mildew inhibitors will protect your investment. Finishes come in clear colors that allow the natural gray of cedar and cypress and

This deck (above and right) combines open areas for sunbathing with a covered balcony for shade or protection from the rain.

HOW DECKS UNITE IRREGULAR FORMS

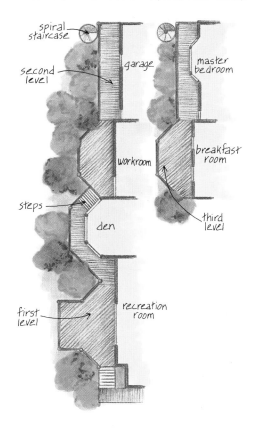

the red of redwood to show through. You can also paint or use an opaque stain for these woods.

By far, the most popular lumber for outdoor projects in the South is pressure-treated pine. This is due to the fact that it is less expensive, readily available, and lasts a long time.

Pressure-treated wood is wood that has had chemical preservatives forced into it under pressure. These preservatives deter microorganisms, as well as termites and other insects, from using the wood as a source of food. This slows decay, making the wood ideal for outdoor use. Depending on the amount of preservative forced into the wood, it can be used above ground, in direct contact with the soil, or even in water. The treatment will not leach into the soil, so it does not endanger your plants.

Although you can often recognize freshly treated wood by its pale green tint, the best identification is by the label or stamp. The stamp will include a number, such as .25 or .40, along with other information. This number, known as the retention level, is an indication of the amount of preservative retained in the wood. A level of .25 indicates that the wood is suitable for use above ground, such as for decking. A rate of .40 means that the wood can be used in contact with the soil and below ground, such as for posts or garden edging. Wood with retention factors as high as 2.5 are available for use in salt water. In general, the higher the number, the greater the retention value.

It is important to determine whether the wood was kiln dried following the treating process. This information is especially significant with decking. Lumber that has not been kiln dried will shrink slightly as it dries naturally. Dried lumber can be spaced 1/8 to 1/4 inch apart, but lumber that has not been dried should be spaced closer to allow for shrinkage.

Wash your hands thoroughly when you finish working with the treated wood. During cleanup, throw scraps in the trash or haul them away. Burning treated wood can be hazardous because of chemicals contained in ashes or smoke. Though pressure-treated wood is ideal for many outdoor projects, it is not recommended for picnic tables or other items likely to come in contact with food.

When your outdoor project is complete, it is time to think about a finish for the wood. Left to weather naturally, pressure-treated pine will eventually turn a soft gray tone. If you prefer to stain or paint the wood, be patient; if done too soon, the result can be cracking and bubbling of the finish as moisture evaporates. It is best to allow wood to weather at least eight weeks before you paint or stain—longer if the weather is damp.

You may want to consider building the supports and frame for your deck out of pressure-treated pine, while using a more expensive wood for the decking, railing, and seating. Also keep in mind that wood comes in different grades, so you may use a lower grade of wood for the infrastructure and a higher grade for the more visible parts of your deck.

For nails, screws, and other fasteners, use hot-dipped galvanized metal. These will resist rust and will not stain the wood. If you cannot find galvanized hardware that suits your taste, be sure that the metal hardware is coated with a rust inhibitor.

The railing (left) looks formal when painted white; when left unpainted (previous page), it suggests simple but stylish craftsmanship.

Decks with unusual shapes, like this spider web (below), are best left to professional carpenters.

If you include a spa on your deck, place it to one side, out of the main traffic area. Partially enclosing it with lattice fencing enhances the cozy feeling.

Left to weather naturally, pressure-treated wood turns a soft gray-brown. The color is particularly handsome for decks that are nestled into wooded sites.

*A terrace beckons irresistibly, calling you to
step outside and enjoy the fruits of your labors
in the garden.*

TERRACES

Whether you call them terraces, patios, or piazzas, their function is much the same as that of a deck. If the terrace is adjacent to the house, however, it is more of a transitional space between indoors and out since a terrace is usually the same level as both the house and garden.

Terraces often are used where a lawn could be used for a similar purpose. However, a lawn requires more time and maintenance to keep it attractive and can frequently be uneven and spongy, making it difficult to set up tables and chairs for entertaining. A terrace guarantees a place for outdoor recreation and reduces the amount of garden maintenance at the same time.

To plan the size and location of your terrace, first identify what purpose it will serve. If it is for entertaining, you will probably want it located

Brick is almost always suitable for terraces—it works with formal or informal houses built of stone, brick, or wood. Small cobblestones (above) provide soft, neutral color that makes a pleasing foil for flowers.

near the living room or family room. For outdoor dining, building the terrace near the dining room or kitchen would be logical. If you simply want a quiet place to read and relax, you may want to have your terrace near a study or bedroom.

When planning the location of your terrace, consider the amount of privacy you will have. Whether you are sunbathing, having morning coffee, or giving a dinner party, you will not want to be on display. Screening the immediate area with trees, shrubs, or a structure can solve this problem. Or you might consider adding a privacy fence, wall, or hedge further out in the garden.

One of the biggest differences between decks and terraces is the material used in their construction. Decks are built of wood, but most terraces are made of stone, brick, concrete, precast pavers, tile, and other forms of masonry.

As you select a material for your terrace, keep in mind maintenance, appearance, and continuity. Be sure the material you choose goes well with your house, especially if the terrace is directly adjacent to the house. Consider using an unusual paving pattern or a combination of different materials for added visual interest.

A terrace does not necessarily have to be flush with the ground. If you have a relatively level site, a sunken or raised terrace is a good way to add variety to the landscape, even if there is as little as one foot difference in elevation. Sunken or raised, you will need to consider drainage. If drainage is a problem, simply sloping a raised terrace will take care of the runoff. For a sunken terrace, you may need to add a drain that connects to an underground drainage system, swale, or sewer.

To avoid the nuisance of dripping water, be aware of gutters and drip lines when planning your terrace. Also pay attention to how the house shades the area. If there is no shade, consider planting trees that will eventually block some sunlight. When doing this, be sure to locate the trees far enough away from the terrace to avoid having the root system buckle the paving. Try to avoid trees that will continually drop leaves or sap. They will make it difficult to keep your terrace clean.

Although the terrace is usually adjacent to the house (right), it can also be tucked into a corner of the garden (below). If you choose this alternative, it is a good idea to use the same material for both the terrace and the paths to it.

Choose The Right Tree
Fast-Growing Trees

(More than 2 feet of growth per year)

Red maple (*Acer rubrum*)—50 to 60 feet*

River birch (*Betula nigra*)—40 to 75 feet

Green ash (*Fraxinus pennsylvanica*)—50 to 60 feet

Thornless honey locust (*Gleditsia triacanthos inermis*)—30 to 60 feet

Tulip poplar (*Liriodendron tulipifera*)—75 to 120 feet

White pine (*Pinus strobus*)—50 to 75 feet

Pin oak (*Quercus palustris*)—60 to 70 feet

Red oak (*Quercus rubra*)—60 to 75 feet

Willow oak (*Quercus phellos*)—50 to 60 feet

Chinese elm (*Ulmus parvifolia*)—40 to 50 feet

Japanese zelkova (*Zelkova serrata*)—50 to 80 feet

Moderate-Growing Trees

(1 to 2 feet of growth per year)

Pecan (*Carya illinoinensis*)—70 to 100 feet

Deodar cedar (*Cedrus deodara*)—40 to 70 feet

Common hackberry (*Celtis occidentalis*)—40 to 60 feet

White ash (*Fraxinus americana*)—50 to 80 feet

Sweet gum (*Liquidambar styraciflua*)—60 to 75 feet

Southern magnolia (*Magnolia grandiflora*)—60 to 80 feet

Water oak (*Quercus nigra*)—50 to 80 feet

Canadian hemlock (*Tsuga canadensis*)—40 to 70 feet

Littleleaf linden (*Tilia cordata*)—60 to 70 feet

Slow-Growing Trees

(less than 1 foot of growth per year)

Sugar maple (*Acer saccharum*)—60 to 75 feet

American beech (*Fagus grandifolia*)—50 to 80 feet

Ginkgo (*Ginkgo biloba*)—50 to 80 feet

Colorado blue spruce (*Picea pungens*)—30 to 60 feet

Longleaf pine (*Pinus palustris*)—25 to 50 feet

White oak (*Quercus alba*)—60 to 100 feet

Live oak (*Quercus virginiana*)—40 to 80 feet

*average mature height

In yards where growing lawn grass might be difficult, a terrace can provide the perfect solution. Massive live oaks shelter this backyard terrace beneath their spreading branches, creating a shady outdoor room. An abundance of container plants introduces color and softens the visual impact of so much concrete.

Bring cooling shade to the terrace with an arbor.

An arbor is a charming alternative to trees for shading your terrace. Even the delicate strips of lattice will filter direct rays from the sun and make summertime on the terrace more pleasant.

If the architectural style of the house allows, you might want to add a canvas awning that can be retracted when not needed. One advantage of an awning is that it offers protection from the rain.

A sense of enclosure is important for a terrace. It enhances the feeling of being in an outdoor room. A low border of shrubs or raised planters is an easy way to accomplish this. As with most small, outdoor spaces, container plants offer a variety of ways to add color and fragrance to your outdoor living area.

Build a sturdy arbor for wisteria: In spring you'll have a fragrant roof overhead, and in summer a leafy canopy will shade you from the sun.

A well-designed arbor can make an architectural statement that is effective even without the drapery of vines. The wooden strips filter the sun, and ceiling fans stir a cooling breeze.

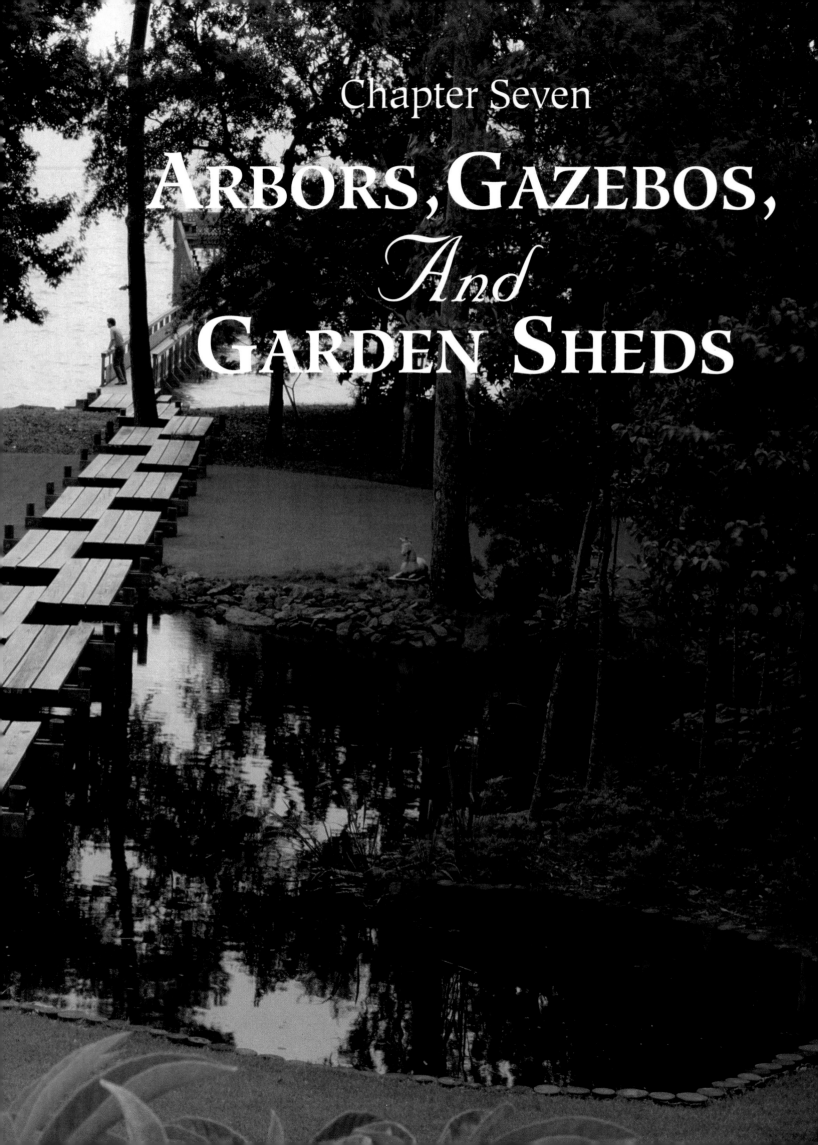

Chapter Seven
ARBORS, GAZEBOS, AND GARDEN SHEDS

C ertain structures, when added to the garden, not only change the way the garden is used but how it is viewed as well. A vine-covered arbor, an ornate gazebo, or a sturdy storage shed all can be attractive additions to your garden while serving very practical purposes.

This arbor (left) emphasizes the fountain as a focal point; while another (right) shades the path between two sunny areas for a more dramatic transition.

ARBORS

There are as many styles of arbors as there are gardens. Whether classical or contemporary in design, an arbor can provide shade and enclosure while linking different areas of the garden. Regardless of function, the arbor's style should be in harmony with the house and garden. A good way to unify the styles is to repeat any interesting architectural details found on the house in your arbor design.

Providing shade is one of the main functions of an arbor. Since there is no solid roof, arbors tend to provide only dappled shade. Growing vines on an arbor will increase the amount of shade provided, while screening wind and rain as well. And if you think that the only place to savor breeze-tossed leaves and fragrant blooms is beneath the limbs of a mature tree, a vine-cloaked arbor can provide the same effect in only a few years. It would take most trees ten years or more to give the same protection and effect.

Since most vines require annual pruning, arbors with vines need to be low enough for safe and efficient maintenance while also allowing plenty of headroom. A height between eight and ten feet is recommended. Also consider the size of the area to be covered, keeping in mind that when a roof is overhead the space tends to feel smaller.

Pressure-treated wood is the most common building material for arbors. It is easy to work with, blends well with the natural elements of the garden, and resists decay. Cedar, redwood, and cypress are also good choices. In some cases, metal pipes or beams or even crossties are well suited for arbors. Whatever you choose, make sure that it is strong and decay resistant.

The most common finishes for arbors are paint, stain, or natural weathering. You will want to finish your arbor in a manner that is compatible with your house. However, if you decide to grow vines on your arbor, you may want to allow the wood to weather naturally since the vine would have to be pulled down each time the arbor is painted or stained.

CHOOSING THE RIGHT VINE

Before you decide on a vine for your arbor, consider its growth habit. This information can prevent a lot of problems later on. For example, small or tightly spaced boards may be pulled apart by a strong, woody vine such as wisteria. On the other hand, yellow jessamine is more delicate and trailing and will benefit from closely spaced supports.

Different types of vines produce different effects. Deciduous vines provide shade in spring and summer yet allow light to filter through during winter months. This is especially beneficial if the arbor is against the house. Evergreen selections form a canopy year-round. Annual vines function much the same as deciduous vines, but you can try a different one when you replant each growing season. Vines with blooms offer an attractive, and often fragrant, bonus.

Most vines will need some help getting started. Attaching the young plant to a support with twist ties or strips of cloth should be sufficient. As the vines grow, some may require seasonal attention to keep them secured or growing in the desired direction.

It's hard to say which comes first, the design of the arbor or the choice of vines. Just be sure the arbor you build is sturdy enough to support the kind of vine you choose.

Selections of Garden Vines

Deciduous Vines

Chinese wisteria (Wisteria sinensis) is covered with fragrant, violet blooms in late spring. It has very strong, woody stems and requires a sturdy structure. White- and pink-blooming selections are also available.

Clematis (Clematis sp.) is available in a wide variety of bloom colors. It grows rapidly and tolerates a variety of climatic conditions. For best results, mulch roots to keep them cool.

Virginia creeper (Parthenocissus quinquefolia) is fast growing and has brilliant scarlet foliage in fall. It prefers full sun and a soil rich in organic matter.

Coral vine (Antigonon leptopus) is a fast-growing vine and has pink flowers in spring. It prefers full sun to light shade.

Evergreen Vines

Yellow jessamine (Gelsemium sempervirens) has an abundance of fragrant, yellow flowers in early spring followed by a lighter, repeat blooming in fall. It prefers full sun or light shade.

Star jasmine (Trachelospermum jasminoides) is a rapid grower with dark green foliage and fragrant, white flowers that bloom in summer. Cut back by a third each fall to promote flowering.

Cross vine (Anisostichus capreolatus) has tube-shaped, yellow-to-red flowers in spring. It will tolerate sun or shade.

Lady Banks rose (Rosa Banksiae) thrives on full sun and poor soil. It will require training because it has no natural means of support. Blooms appear in late spring.

Annual Vines

Common morning glory (Impomoea purpurea) will grow up to forty feet in a single season and offers white-to-blue flowers. Technically an annual, it often reseeds.

Sweet pea (Lathyrus odoratus) is a fragrant and colorful spring-blooming vine that prefers full sun.

Black-eyed Susan vine (Thunbergia alata) offers a profusion of yellow flowers. Plant in early spring in full sun.

Cup-and-saucer vine (Cobaea scandens) has purple blooms that last from summer to mid-fall. It may act as a perennial in warmer regions of the South.

Gazebos may conjure up romantic images of moonlit nights and poetry, but their function is often a bit more practical.

GAZEBOS

Gazebos offer a sheltered outdoor setting for entertaining and relaxing. They have been used for centuries as outdoor oases. You can find them in the garden designs of the Far East, Great Britain, and certainly here in America. Though they enjoyed their greatest surge of popularity during the Victorian era, there is no need to limit your design options to that style.

The Victorian-style gazebo is certainly a favorite, but there are a variety of other designs to choose from which will complement the style of your home and garden. Chippendale, contemporary, lath-house, rustic, and open-air are just a few of the choices available. Each of these styles can be designed to accommodate large groups, or the designs adapt easily to suit a cozy crowd of two. The size can be dictated by your intended use.

Gazebos, or summer houses as they are sometimes called, may be equipped with ceiling fans, wet bars, barbecue grills, lights, and sound. These structures are the hub of activity during pleasant weather. Or for a smaller space, you may simply hang a hammock for a quiet place to nap or read.

The route to and from your gazebo will need your attention also. A free-standing gazebo certainly will be enjoyed more often if the pathway leading to it is appealing, comfortable, and easily marked.

The key factors in choosing the materials for your gazebo are compatibility, durability, and

This spacious gazebo, with its domical roof and cupola, combines the benefits of a deck or terrace as a place for outdoor living with the advantages of shade, shelter, and a feeling of privacy.

This gazebo (above) is simply a roof over a deck, but a ceiling fan makes it comfortable through the summer, and concealed lighting means it can be used for nighttime entertaining. The style of a gazebo should complement the house: Nestled into its rural setting, this gazebo (right) recalls the tin-roofed, Greek Revival-style farmhouses that dot the Southeast.

Lattice panels decorate opposite corners, adding a touch of style and a sense of enclosure.

availability. For roofing, you will probably want to use asphalt shingles or whatever was used to roof your house. The repetition of materials enhances the harmony between the house and garden.

A simple approach to adding a gazebo to your garden is to start with a prefabricated gazebo and dress it up with custom details to suit your needs and style. Simply adding a molding or decorative trim can turn a plain structure into one uniquely suited to your garden. Repeating fence, railing, or molding details that are used in other parts of the garden is a good way to unify the elements.

GARDEN SHEDS

It is amazing how quickly you can surround yourself with a staggering array of tools, not to mention sacks of peat moss, fertilizer, and seed. Sooner or later any avid gardener is going to face the challenge of storing these tools and supplies. The garage is often the answer, but a storage shed built specifically for garden tools and supplies can be a practical solution and a handsome addition to the garden.

A primary consideration for such a structure is ease of access. Most likely, the shed will store frequently used equipment, so it is better if you do not have to go to the furthermost reaches of the garden to retrieve a trowel. A location

near the house or active area of gardening is ideal. However, if your structure is purely utilitarian, you may prefer to nestle it away from outdoor entertainment areas.

To dress up a standard prefabricated shed, consider painting the structure to help it blend into the garden. Adding a window or decorative door also gives a fresh look to a plain design.

Garden sheds are available in prefabricated metal styles, wood kits, and custom wood designs. The style you choose will depend on how visible your shed will be and the use you have in mind. Regardless of the style, it is a good idea to make the shed bigger than you think you will need—a shed can fill up and become cramped very quickly.

A garden shed can be simple and small (left), or roomy and sophisticated-looking (below). But while you're building, why not plan for extra space to accommodate a potting bench and work space (right)?

You can give a prefabricated shed a custom-designed look by installing windows and decorative doors. Shutters, window boxes, and carriage lights (above) complete the disguise.

Chapter Eight
POOLS, FOUNTAINS, AND PONDS

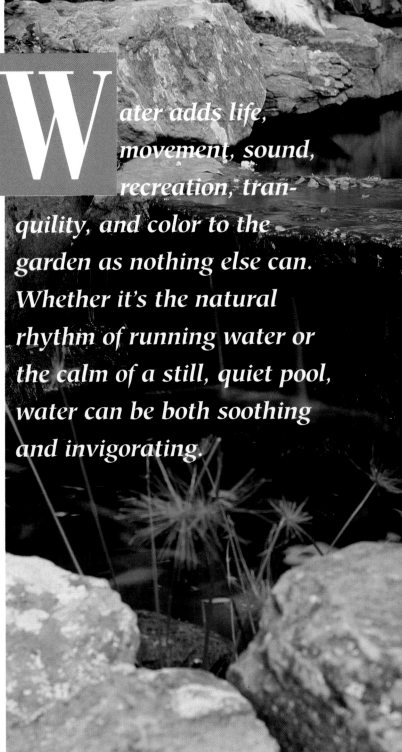

W ater adds life, movement, sound, recreation, tranquility, and color to the garden as nothing else can. Whether it's the natural rhythm of running water or the calm of a still, quiet pool, water can be both soothing and invigorating.

With its cherub fountain and formal design, this elegant setting for swimming feels like a little bit of Europe transplanted to the South. Ivy cloaks the retaining wall and tumbles over the top, helping to cool the effect of so much brick.

SWIMMING POOLS

Once reserved as a luxury for the elite, swimming pools are becoming more attainable. With such a wide range of styles and prices available, it is much easier to add a pool to your garden.

Though usually thought of as a spot for warm-weather recreation, a swimming pool dominates the landscape year-round. If designed properly, this can be a tremendous asset. However, if proper attention is not given to the style, size, and maintenance requirements of the pool, you could have a real garden eyesore. A poorly designed or positioned pool is very difficult to play down.

There are many factors to consider when building a swimming pool, from the purpose of the pool, its size, location, and cost, to safety and maintenance. When it comes to actually designing a pool, the shapes and styles available are endless, and there are many different finishes and features to consider. Think the entire project through before beginning any construction. If you plan to eventually add a pool, make it a part of the master plan, even if you do not install it for several years. That way you will not build a terrace in what would have been the perfect spot for the pool.

PLANNING YOUR POOL

Think about your reasons for wanting a pool. If the pool is for your children, who will presumably one day move away, will you still want to maintain a pool? In such a case, you may want to consider an above-ground pool that can be removed.

You may want a pool for sunbathing. But pools are not essential for sunbathing. You may want a pool for recreation. You may want to swim laps. Each of these valid reasons for having a pool come with their own set of options and criteria. Before embarking on a pool design, be sure that you have looked at all the possibilities and have a purpose for the structure in mind.

Once you are convinced that a pool is truly what you want, the next consideration is size. This will be guided by the purpose. Lap pools will need to be as long as possible and the width can be as narrow as five feet. If you expect more than four

A stepped bridge across the pool allows headroom for swimmers. Visually, it repeats the stepped terrace that integrates this pool into the design of the house.

If your pool is likely to become the focus of summertime entertaining, be sure to make the decking roomy enough for tables, chairs, and chaise longues.

This pool is private, thanks to the courtyard wall. Extending the roof beams makes the pool feel like it is indoors.

people at a time to use a pool, the size should reflect that. If it is simply a pool to cool off in or to float one or two rafts in, then it can be much smaller.

There are no set rules about the dimensions of a pool. A wide range of predesigned pools are available at most pool companies. They may or may not have the right design for you. Just keep in mind that there may be a difference in cost between what the pool companies offer and what you want. Even if there is a cost difference, weigh the value of getting the right design for your garden against the savings being offered, especially when you spread the cost over the life of the pool.

When determining size, consider both depth and surface area. This is especially important if you want to dive into the pool or if you

would like to be able to use it for water sports. If the pool does not need to be deep, you are better off leaving it shallow. This will reduce cost and maintenance and make the pool safer.

Next you must decide where to put the pool. At the same scale as your site analysis (see chapter 1), draw a rectangle or other form that approximates the square footage you want. Using your site analysis, note the locations which lend themselves to a pool site. The more level a place is the better, as it will reduce the amount of grading required. Take into consideration the amount of sunlight the area receives. Usually this will mean few or no trees overhead to drop debris into the pool. You may prefer a location that gets some afternoon shade on part of the pool area.

For an in-ground pool, you will have to be clear of any underground utilities, as well as any roots of large trees you plan to keep. You will also need to consider where the pool pumps and filters will be located, keeping in mind that the price increases with the distance from the pool. Plan on additional storage for other pool-related items such as floats, chemicals, and tools.

Other factors in deciding on a location include visibility and accessibility. Can a view of the pool be enjoyed from inside the house? Do you want to be able to see the pool from inside the home for aesthetic or safety reasons? Is the location convenient to the house, or do you have to cross the lot? Sometimes the best location for building the pool is not the most convenient. Also note any plants

The design possibilities for in-ground pools are nearly limitless. The only constraints are the site you have available and your budget.

that would have to be removed in the process of construction.

POOL SAFETY

With a site located, you will need to consider safety. Despite the pleasure you may derive from it, a pool is a potential hazard. You must be able to supervise children in or near the pool and keep them away from it if you cannot supervise them. Check with the local health department or zoning board to determine what pool safety regulations exist for your community. Be sure to check the minimum fence heights and any other restrictions.

Most cities require you to fence a pool area for safety reasons. The gate should be self-closing and self-latching, with the lock out of reach of young children. If you have an above-ground pool, be able to remove or block the ladder or steps that lead up to the pool. If your entire garden is already fenced in, you may not have to add another fence immediately around the pool. Most cities have a minimum distance from the water's edge to the fence.

Other safety concerns include visibility from other areas of the garden and the material used around the pool. Also check on insurance coverage and liability.

The fencing around a pool follows the same principles of design you use elsewhere in the garden. Since the pool is often a popular gathering place, appearance becomes even more important. With a bit of creativity, safety fencing

can enhance the beauty of the pool area while satisfying safety requirements.

POOL MAINTENANCE

With an idea of the type and size pool you want, you can begin to get an idea about the amount of maintenance involved. Depending upon how much money you want to spend, a pool can take a lot of your time or very little. There are many machines, attachments, cleaning systems, and services available to assist you. However, there is a price to pay for that luxury. Most people seek a happy medium whereby a filter system keeps the water clean and an automated pool cleaner works around the clock. This still requires the periodic addition of chemicals, hand-skimming, vacuuming, and some scrubbing.

One feature that impacts both safety and maintenance is a pool cover. A safety cover is designed to withstand the weight of a child or dog walking across it. A standard maintenance cover is not as sturdy and is designed primarily to keep debris from falling in the pool. These covers are usually on a roller that is either hand cranked or motor driven. They are especially useful during stormy times of the year, leaf-dropping time in fall, or to cover the pool for the winter. In some cities, a pool cover can take the place of a safety fence. If considering this as an option, keep in mind that you will be required to uncover and recover the pool each time you

use it to ensure safety. Also be aware that a covered pool has a very different look than an uncovered one. If the view of the pool is of special importance, even during winter months, this option may not be for you.

TYPES OF POOLS

Pools are broken down into two main categories: in-ground and above-ground. In-ground is by far the most popular and is built so that the water level of the finished pool is about the same as the surrounding topography. This usually requires a substantial amount of excavation.

The most popular type of in-ground pool is made of sprayed concrete called Gunite. It offers the greatest amount of flexibility in design. These pools are formed by excavating a hole, building a frame, adding steel reinforcing bars, then spraying the concrete mixture over the frame. The pool is then finished with a coat of plaster for a smooth texture. Besides the durability of the concrete shell, the biggest advantage to using this method is that you can create any shape imaginable.

Another popular type, for reasons of economy and maintenance, is the vinyl-liner pool. This type of pool uses thick vinyl supported by a frame made of aluminum, masonry, wood, or plastic. If protected from the sun and otherwise maintained, vinyl liners can last up to ten years before they need replacing. Meanwhile, should a tear occur, it can usually be repaired without draining the pool. Vinyl-lined pools are durable and handsome. One drawback to this type of pool is that it is more difficult to custom design.

Precast fiberglass shells come in a variety of forms. If you do not necessarily require a custom design, this may be a good type of pool for you. Since these pools are lowered into the ground by a crane, you must have adequate access to the pool area. The chief advantage of this type of pool is the ease of cleaning. The smooth surface slows down algae growth and makes removal a cinch.

Above-ground pools tend to cost substantially less than in-ground models. An above-ground pool is an aluminum or steel structure with a vinyl liner. The shape of an above-ground pool is typically limited to either a circle, oval, square, or rectangle. Some above-ground pools are not vinyl lined, instead they are supported by retaining walls. With decking and plants around the edge, an above-ground pool is an attractive garden addition.

Pool Shapes and Styles

Pool shapes can vary widely. Rectangular, oval, square, kidney-shaped, angular, free-form, and round are some of the more common forms. The shape and style of your pool needs to reflect your garden's style. If you have a Colonial-style home and a formal planting, then you will probably want a formal-looking pool. From a design standpoint, however, a contemporary home may not accommodate a formal pool.

Tinting the bottom of the swimming pool is an effective way to soften its impact on the landscape. Darker colors, such as navy, charcoal, or deep green, tend to fade and blend into the landscape better. They also increase the reflective quality of the water. The best time to stain is when you plaster the pool. If you already have a pool and are interested in doing this, consider adding a stain when you replaster, or use an epoxy paint over the existing plaster.

(Left and previous pages) Tinting the bottom of the pool dark blue or charcoal helps blend it into the landscape so that it becomes a pleasing garden feature as well as a place for recreation.

As you design the pool, remember to design the area around it too, so that both fit comfortably into the landscape.

AROUND THE POOL

This area is generally referred to as pool decking. The purpose of decking is to provide a place to enjoy the pool and to create a buffer to keep debris and insects out of the pool. Sometimes the purpose is simply to be able to get around the pool as you clean it.

If you want a pathway to go around the perimeter of the pool, you will need at least three feet of paving. Plan on at least eight feet to accommodate sunbathers, while leaving room for foot traffic. It is a good idea to have a gathering area, as you will inevitably want to have a party by the pool. Some pools may be tucked into such tight spaces that there is no room to walk around the edge. In a case such as this, be sure to consider how you will be able to maintain the pool. From both a safety and maintenance standpoint, you should be able to reach any point in the pool with a skimmer or pole.

The choice of decking material depends on safety and expense, but the style of decking should be in harmony with the rest of the materials in the garden. If stone is a dominant feature in the landscape, you may want to consider using it as decking. Stone may look out of place if brick is the most dominant element. Wood decking is a good choice if the pool is above ground.

Be sure any material you use around the pool is slip-resistant. The majority of pool-related accidents involve people slipping and falling, so you will want a textured surface. Smooth tile and concrete can be very slippery when wet. Be certain the area around the pool drains well so as to avoid puddles of standing water. Make sure that the water drains away from the pool, not into it. This will significantly reduce maintenance.

The point where the pool meets the decking is called the coping. The coping forms a border or edge and can add an attractive, finished look to the design. The same can be said of the trim tile that extends from the coping to the water line or just below. This combination of materials offers endless ways to dress up the pool. Brightly colored ceramic tiles or a continuation of the decking materials are but two of hundreds of approaches to this finishing touch. For safety reasons, a rolled edge on the coping is recommended.

Plants at the water's edge give a lush, exotic look to the pool area. They can be added simply by designing planting pockets around the edge of the pool. It is better to include this type of design decision during the planning stages, rather than deciding later. Make sure that there is adequate drainage where you plant, and avoid plants that have an extremely aggressive root system which could whittle away at the pool wall. If you already have the pool in place, add plants in containers. The plants you select need to be able to tolerate high light intensity due to the reflective quality of the water.

Man-made stone rings the spa (above) and makes a natural-looking foreground for lush plantings of areca palm and silver buttonwood. Beds of lantana soften the pool's edge.

FINISHING TOUCHES

As you plan your pool and surrounding area, remember the pool equipment. Keeping this conglomeration of pumps and tanks out of sight will make your pool area much more beautiful. Often you have little choice where the pump and filter are installed. Power and water lines, as well as the site of the pool, may determine the location of the equipment for you. Sometimes everything will fit into a garage or carport, but frequently the equipment must be separate from the house. A wood screen, evergreen hedge, or a pool shed offer attractive solutions to this problem.

If the pool area is to be used at night, you will need to add outdoor lighting. Lighting a pool area requires that both the pool and the surrounding decking be lit. Once again, it is much better to include lighting to your initial plan for the pool area. Underwater pool lights are difficult to add to a finished pool.

SPAS AND HOT TUBS

Hot tubs and spas are joining swimming pools in popularity for outdoor water recreation. It is not unusual to see a spa designed in conjunction with a swimming pool, though it can work beautifully as a separate feature as well. Hot tubs are self-supporting structures.

If you want both a spa and a swimming pool, you often can build both together for less money than building them separately. The primary consideration when having a spa built in with the pool is keeping the heated water of the spa separate from the pool water. Building a common underwater wall for both the pool and spa is one way to accomplish this. Having the spa adjacent but completely separate from the pool is another good solution.

Hot tubs usually are round and have a barrel-like appearance. This makes them especially well suited for being set into decks. The tubs range from five to six feet or more in diameter and are

usually about two to four feet deep. The biggest advantage of hot tubs is that they are relatively portable and do not require any excavation. They do not offer much flexibility in design, however, and being made of wood, they are not as durable as fiberglass or masonry spas.

When determining where in the garden to place a spa or hot tub, consider privacy, sunlight and shade, wind, safety, ease of access, and how the structure will blend with the rest of the garden. You will also need to check how local building restrictions pertain to these features.

The pool and spa combination (previous pages and above right) is often easier and more economical to build than installing them separately. If the spa stands alone, however, there is no problem with keeping the heated water from mixing with the cooler water of the pool (right).

Pool Coping And Decking

A coping of tan tiles makes a smooth edge to sit on. Mottled blue and tan ceramic tile accents the step risers and the water line.

Water spills over this raised black-tile edge into a shallow trough between the tile and the surrounding textured-concrete deck. (From there, the water is pumped back into the pool.)

Concrete decking has been cut to accommodate the irregular forms of the stone coping. Dark blue tile below the coping creates the effect of a velvety shadow.

Aggregate decking and brick coping provide slip-resistant surfaces. Terra-cotta trim tile below the coping harmonizes with the earth tones of these materials.

FOUNTAINS

Fountains offer something to the garden that has no equal—moving water. The random splashing of a single jet, the soothing, steady stream of a waterfall, or the ever-changing dance of time-controlled jets, all add song, movement, and life to the garden. Fountains can be used as a focal point, garden ornament, or as a way to muffle undesirable noises.

If you decide to add a fountain to your garden, you will have a lot of styles from which to choose. Whether your fountain is custom-made or ready-built, it needs to fit in well with the existing garden. It likely will be the center of attention, not only for the sound of the water but for its sculptural beauty.

Among your choices are fountains that hang on walls and are self-contained and recirculating, or elaborate operations with multiple jets. Many different kits are available that allow you to do your own installation, but the most common and adaptable is a vessel, or body of water, with a single jet rising up out of it. Most pumps and jets allow you to control the jet from a slow gentle bubble to a high-reaching stream that splashes down hard upon its return to the basin.

As you determine the right jets for your fountain and setting, both size and sound should be considered. If you are using a narrow or small base, the stream should probably not be a tall one. If the jet height exceeds twice the diameter of the base, the stream may look out of proportion. And while the sound of the splashing water is soothing and can drown out undesirable sounds, you do not want it to be overbearing. This is true particularly for fountains used in courtyards or other enclosed spaces where the sound will be amplified.

A lion's head is an ancient motif for fountains. The sound of the fountain (right) is multiplied as water spills from the basin to another pool below.

$\mathcal{M}$ake Your Own Garden Fountain

Water features do not have to be expensive. The simple one pictured here costs under $100 and takes less than an hour to make. All you need is a container, pump, sealer, and a grounded electrical plug.

Start by purchasing a concrete planter with a drain hole in the bottom; then coat the inside of the planter with a water sealer. This keeps the concrete from absorbing water, which in turn prevents cracking during a freeze.

You will then need to purchase a small submersible pump. The pump size you select will depend upon the vessel you use and the desired effect. Your local garden center or home center should carry these and can advise you on what size to buy.

If you have an outdoor electrical outlet for the pump, you can have a simple pot fountain.

You will need to cut off the plug from the end of the pump cord, set the pump in the planter, and run the cord through the drain hole.

Make sure there is enough cord inside the planter to give the pump the desired height; then use a cork to plug the drain hole and hold the cord in place. Seal the inside and outside of the hole with silicone (available at most hardware stores). Attach a new plug to the end of the cord.

After letting the silicone set overnight, place the finished fountain in your garden, add gravel to adjust the height of the jet, fill the container with water, and plug in the cord. Now sit back and enjoy the wonderful sound of water.

CHIPMUNK
CROSSING

REFLECTING POOLS AND PONDS

As Herman Melville wrote, "meditation and water are wedded forever." Whether your pool is naturalistic (previous pages) or formal (above), spellbinding reflections are yours for the looking.

A reflecting pool or pond provides a tranquil, soothing element in the garden, as well as a home for water plants and fish. These pools and ponds possess a meditative and reflective quality all their own, quite different from a fountain or swimming pool.

When considering a feature like this, first decide if it is to be in a private or open area. This will determine whether it should be placed near a deck or terrace or tucked into a more secluded part of the garden. Find a location that is fairly level, since the rim of the pond itself needs to be level. If you want a water garden, look for a sunny spot as most water plants prefer full sun.

After you have chosen a location, decide on the shape. Whether using a flexible liner, fiberglass shell, or a concrete basin, you can create almost any form, as long as it is compatible with the surrounding landscape. The edging around the pool or pond can help set the style. For both formal and natural-looking ponds, a variety of materials are available for edging. Stone and rough-cut pavers give a natural look, while more refined materials, such as brick and granite, lend sophistication.

Once you have decided on the size and shape of the pool, you can buy the liner, pump, and filter. If you want the pool to double as a fountain, use a pump with variable pressure so that you can regulate the height of the spray. Be sure that the pump you choose has the capacity to recirculate all of the water in the pond at least once in three hours. This is essential if your pond has plants and fish.

ADDING PLANTS AND FISH
Once the water in a pond is dechlorinated, it will be safe for fish and plants. Whether purchased locally or by mail order, they should come with complete instructions on care. Be sure to follow the directions carefully for best results.

The two main categories of water plants for the South are water lilies and bog plants. Lilies produce colorful, showy blossoms and have flat, round leaves floating on the water. Bog plants are primarily foliage plants such as cattail and canna, but water iris are also included in this group.

When choosing plants for your pond, consider your climate, pool size, plant maintenance, and the look you want. The most common source for water plants is through mail-order catalogs, but there will be less trauma to plants if you can buy them locally.

A garden inspired by Japanese designs presents a landscape in miniature, with water as a central feature.

NATURAL WATER FEATURES

You may be fortunate enough to have a natural water feature on your property. Perhaps a stream runs through your garden or you border a lake or river. Before you build near a river or lake, be aware of any laws that govern how close to the water's edge you are allowed to build and whether or not you can alter or obstruct the flow of water.

For streams, you might want to consider shoring up the edges to keep the water where you want it and to avoid erosion during heavy rains. Planting water-loving plants, such as weeping willow, river birch, and ferns, is another way to capitalize on what you have from both an aesthetic and erosion point of view. You might consider designing a garden path with a bridge that crosses the stream to show off a view or an attractive planting. Having a gathering area or getaway on the far side of a stream heightens the sense of seclusion and privacy, while taking full advantage of the natural setting.

If you're lucky enough to have a stream running through your yard, make the most of it. This stream (left), lush with ferns, has been carefully embellished to look like the work of nature, not man. Although stone retaining walls channel the water flow (right) into a more artificial course, a stone bridge and water-loving plants help make it an attractive feature.

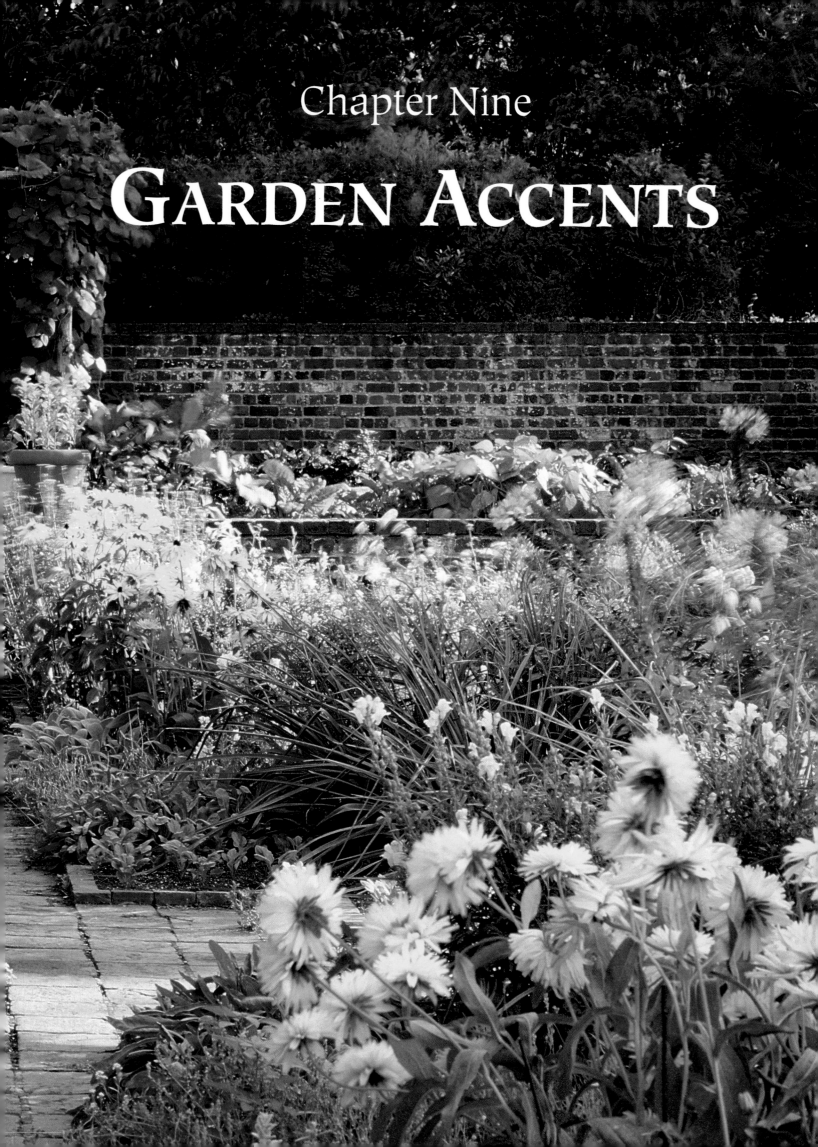

Chapter Nine

GARDEN ACCENTS

fter the planning and work are done, it's time to add the accents that make your garden unique; these are the personal touches that reflect your taste and interests.

It can be a single sculpture, a bench in your favorite part of the garden, or a birdhouse for feathered friends. Rather than detract from the existing design, garden accents should complement and refine what is already there.

SCULPTURE AND GARDEN ORNAMENTS

One of the best reasons for sculpture in the garden is for accent or emphasis. Sculpture lends itself readily to being a focal point and in most cases serves that purpose very well. Another important element of sculpture is surprise. For instance, you might happen upon a statue of Pan playing a silent tune while perched on a rock. Or you may spot a terra-cotta rabbit, partly concealed under a bush, its ears erect as if startled. Beside a path, a little girl, cast in lead, stands amid the flowers. Small details such as these give a garden personality.

Garden shops and mail-order catalogs feature a vast selection of outdoor ornaments—urns, fountains, plaques, statuary, birdbaths, finials, wind chimes, and more. Just remember that restraint is the key to success with ornaments. The effect is diminished if you use too many.

Many inexpensive garden ornaments are made of concrete, which weathers to a mellow gray. Hand-carved stone ornaments are extremely durable but can be expensive. Stone pieces made by molding finely ground marble, limestone, and rock are a less expensive substitute for hand-carved ornaments. The molded stone pieces look and weather like natural stone and hold up extremely well. Beautiful terra-cotta pieces, whether imported or made of clay, add a rich, earthy look to the garden. Because terra-cotta is porous, it is subject to cracking in cold, wet weather and probably is better suited to warm regions.

A statue of Pan is just the right size to perch on a rock.

A statue can serve as a visual anchor in a flower bed that changes with the seasons. Cast in lead, this little girl with her umbrella stands amid the sedum.

The most popular metals used for ornaments are iron, lead, copper, and bronze. Iron stands up well to variations in heat and cold, but it will rust if not painted. Lead pieces are practically maintenance free, but they may soften in the hot sun. Copper develops a light green film of verdigris over time, which contrasts beautifully with the darker green of many plants. And sunlight striking the surface of a bronze piece illuminates the landscape with a warm glow.

A tile-and-wrought-iron table under an arbor is the perfect place to show off a collection of favorite things.

For a really distinctive accent, look for pieces by contemporary artists. This whimsical copper chicken brings lots of personality to a corner of the garden.

This planter appears to be as old and weathered as the mossy wall it adorns, when in fact, it is a new concrete piece painted to look like lead.

Paint Concrete For The Look Of Lead

Lead garden ornaments not only endure, they get better with age. However, lead ornaments are costly and often hard to find. Meanwhile, you will find a variety of reasonably priced pieces cast in concrete, and following the step-by-step instructions given here, you can have the look of lead for the price of concrete.

The key to this illusion is to choose an ornament that looks like it could be made of lead. Some concrete ornaments may have a rough surface. Look for one that is as smooth as possible for the best effect.

For best results, use a water-based exterior paint and paint the piece on a warm, dry day. The paint soaks into the grain and dries in about five minutes. Do not put polyurethane over the paint; that gives it too much sheen. Use an earthy, yellow-gray putty color and a dark, charcoal shade to achieve a truly lead-like appearance.

For containers, seal the inside with a concrete water sealant or melted paraffin. If the container is large, line it with a plastic pot and pack mulch between the two.

Step 1: Mix half putty-colored paint with half water; paint liberally on the concrete. Allow it to drip, then dry.

Step 2: Mix half gray and half water. Paint this on, letting it puddle and run down. Let it dry.

Step 3: Mix equal parts putty, gray, and water. Paint and sponge this on, but before it dries completely, wipe it off. Let paint remain in the crevices of the piece. If this coat does not wipe off easily, use a moist rag.

Step 4: You can continue to refine the finish by retouching with putty or gray on a damp rag. This extra step makes the finish more complex. When paint is completely dry, use a soft rag to polish it a bit.

There's no danger of this snail devouring the flowers. For the best effect, place sculptures of garden creatures in settings that their live counterparts would enjoy.

Variegated ivy trained to a form in a terra-cotta pot makes a striking vertical accent at the end of a path.

Just as paintings give character to a room, so can plaques enliven vine-covered walls.

Urns are among the most popular garden accents, combining sculptural form with function as a planter. A miniature garden of succulents thrives in the one opposite.

One really spectacular element, like this fountain, can define the character of the whole garden.

This birdbath was a particularly happy choice for the fountain: The scroll at the back of the shell shape subtly imitates the C-shaped curve of the pool.

LIGHTING

Lighting the garden allows you to enjoy it whenever you please. Lights also provide a safety feature for driveways, parking areas, walkways, pool areas, and entries. Soft, subtle lighting can be a very effective security measure. You can wire the lights easily to timers, so the lights come on even if you are not at home.

There are several styles of night lighting. Downlighting most closely resembles natural lighting and is the most common technique for lighting walks and drives. Downlighting can be accomplished with small fixtures a foot or two above ground that light only the immediate area or by lights in nearby trees that illuminate a broader area.

This same technique is employed in what is referred to as moonlighting. This involves having downlights set high in the trees to give the effect of moonlight shining down and casting shadows on the ground. Uplights are placed a few feet below the downlights to illuminate the tree foliage and mask the source of the downlight.

Uplighting simply means a light that is placed at the base of a tree, wall, or sculpture and

Lighting makes a walkway safer at night, but if you choose fanciful fixtures like this one, it becomes a delightful garden accent.

shines upward. This is most effective when showcasing an object or plant with a particularly sculptural form. Uplighting often is used to silhouette a tree against a wall.

Accent lighting can be as bold as a spotlight or as subtle as tiny, twinkle lights. Accent lights are purely for ambience and may be reserved for entertaining or other special occasions.

OUTDOOR FIREPLACES

Outdoor fireplaces add character and warmth to the garden. Simply build a fireplace or firepit outdoors, shelter it, and you have an outdoor room with lots of atmosphere. In fact, it is the open-air quality that is most appealing. Outdoor spaces with fireplaces can serve the same function as a den, with the added novelty of being outdoors.

Fireplaces provide more than ambience. They provide heat, which can be a great asset when used in conjunction with a swimming pool. A warm fire is a welcome site to a swimmer on a cool

A fire pit has no chimney and should be located away from the house.

evening. A fireplace can extend the swimming season from early spring into fall.

With few exceptions, indoor and outdoor fireplaces are built the same way. One exception is a fire pit. This is a masonry structure designed for open fires and has no chimney. This type of outdoor fireplace should be located away from the house to avoid problems with smoke.

When choosing the location for a fireplace with a chimney, be sure it can be seen and enjoyed from the house as well as from the garden. This will satisfy both aesthetic and safety functions. The chimney also can be used to screen unsightly views. Avoid obstructions, such as overhanging limbs, which pose a fire hazard.

An outdoor fireplace provides cozy ambience, turning a covered terrace into an outdoor den.

SCREENS

After all of your planning and design work, you still may have areas that need to be screened from view. They may be additions such as pool equipment, a storage area, or your neighbor's doghouse. If you are faced with a view that needs to be blocked or protected, consider adding a screen.

Screens can be freestanding or attached to another structure, such as the house, deck, or an arbor. Screens do not have to form a solid barrier, often a lattice panel is sufficient to obscure the view while not closing off an area visually. You also may consider using canvas as a screen if it suits the style of your house and garden.

Prefabricated or custom-designed and built, wooden lattice may be one of the most popular materials for screening. One drawback is that it does not last a long time. Ten years is its average life span. Lattice made of PVC is becoming more readily available and looks identical to the wood version. It does not take paint or stain but comes in several colors and will last indefinitely.

Lattice was used here to hide ugly porch supports and provide a place for vines to climb.

A lattice panel is a good choice for blocking the air-conditioning unit from view. Paint the lattice the same color as the house and disguise with airy, low-growing plants to make it look like part of the foundation.

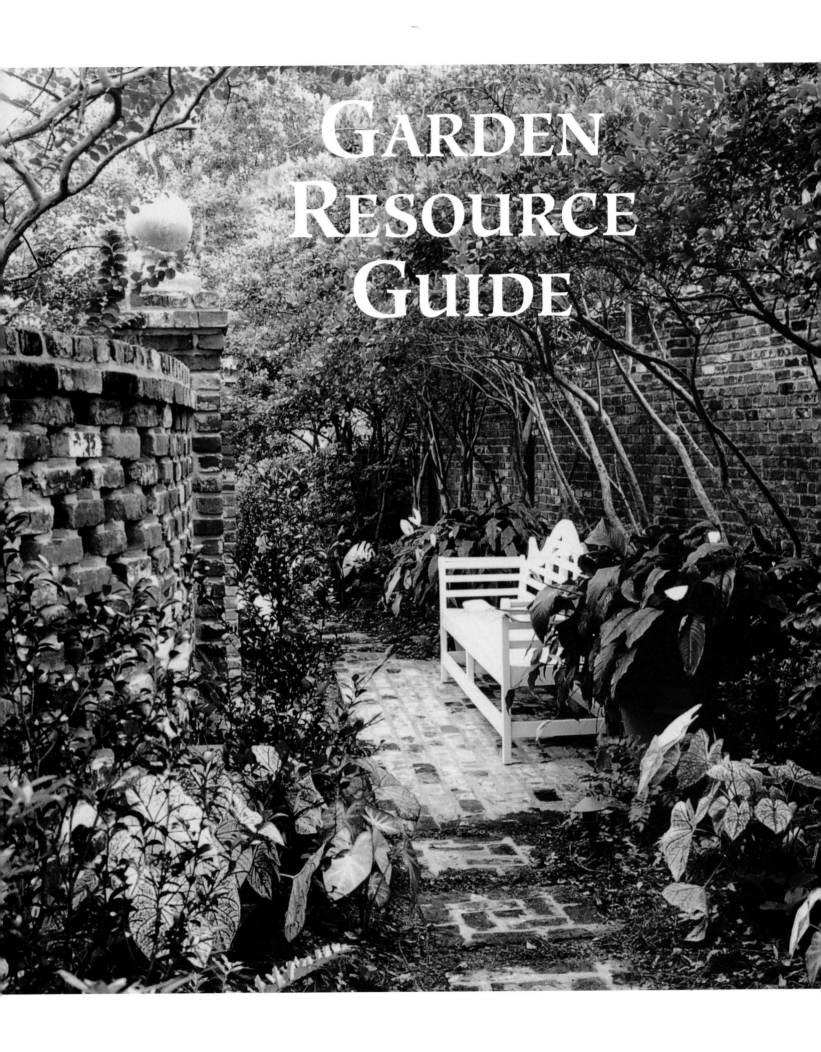

GARDEN
RESOURCE
GUIDE

*Following are some mail-order resources
which will help you create the garden
of your dreams.*

ARBORS

Kinsman Company, Inc.
River Road
Point Pleasant, PA 18950
(215) 297-5613

Sun Designs
P.O. Box 206
173 E. Wisconsin Avenue
(Oconomowoc)
Delafield, WI 53018-0206
(414) 567-4255

BIRD FEEDERS AND FOOD

Hastings
P.O. Box 115535
Atlanta, GA 30310-8535
(404) 755-6580, or
(800) 334-1771

Lazy Hill Farm Designs
P.O. Box 235
Colerain, NC 27924
(919) 356-2828

BIRDHOUSES

Gardener's Eden
Box 7307
San Francisco, CA 94120-7307
(415) 428-9292 or 421-4242

The Walt Nicke Company
P.O. Box 433
36 McLeod Lane
Topsfield, MA 01983
(508) 887-3388

Winterthur Museum &
Gardens
Catalogue Division
102 Enterprise Place
Dover, DE 19735
(302) 678-9200 or
(800) 767-0500

FISH FOR GARDEN PONDS

Lilypons Water Gardens
P.O. Box 10
6800 Lilypons Road
Lilypons, MD 21717-0010
(301) 874-5133

Perry's Water Gardens
191 Leatherman Gap Road
Franklin, NC 28734
(704) 524-3264 or 369-5648

Van Ness Water Gardens
2460 N. Euclid
Upland, CA 91786-1199
(714) 982-2425

FOUNTAINS

Garden Magic
2001-1/2 Fairview Road
Raleigh, NC 27608
(919) 833-7315

Lilypons Water Gardens
P.O. Box 10
6800 Lilypons Road
Lilypons, MD 21717-0010
(301) 874-5133

Robinson Iron
P.O. Drawer 1235
Robinson Road
Alexander City, AL 35010
(205) 329-8486

Tilley's Nursery/The Water-
Works
111 E. Fairmount Street
Coopersburg, PA 18036
(215) 282-4784

GARDEN BENCHES

Brandywine Garden Furniture
24 Phoenixville Pike
Malvern, PA 19355
(215) 640-1212 or
(800) 722-5434

Charleston Battery Bench, Inc.
191 King Street
Charleston, SC 29401
(803) 722-3842

The Garden Concepts
Collection
P.O. Box 241233
Memphis, TN 38124-1233
(901) 756-1649

Garden Magic
2001-1/2 Fairview Road
Raleigh, NC 27608
(919) 833-7315

John Deere Catalog
1400 Third Avenue
Moline, IL 61265
(800) 544-2122

Reed Bros.
Turner Station
Sebastopol, CA 95472
(707) 795-6261

Robinson Iron
P.O. Drawer 1235
Robinson Road
Alexander City, AL 35010
(205) 329-8486

Smith and Hawken
25 Corte Madera
Mill Valley, CA 94941
(415) 383-8070 or 383-4415

Van Klassens Fine Garden
Furniture
4619B Central Avenue Road
Knoxville, TN 37912
(615) 688-2565

GARDEN FURNITURE

Brandywine Garden Furniture
24 Phoenixville Pike
Malvern, PA 19355
(215) 640-1212 or
(800) 722-5434

Charleston Battery Bench, Inc.
191 King Street
Charleston, SC 29401
(803) 722-3842

The Clapper Co.
1121 Washington Street
West Newton, MA 02165
(617) 244-7900

Gardener's Eden
Box 7307
San Francisco, CA 94120-7307
(415) 428-9292 or 421-4242

Park Place
2251 Wisconsin Avenue, N.W.
Washington, D.C. 20007
(202) 342-6294

The Plow & Hearth
301 Madison Road
Orange, VA 22960
(703) 672-1712 or
(800) 527-5247

Reed Bros.
Turner Station
Sebastopol, CA 95472
(707) 795-6261
FAX (707)829-8620

Robinson Iron
P.O. Drawer 1235
Robinson Road
Alexander City, AL 35010
(205) 329-8486

Smith and Hawken
25 Corte Madera
Mill Valley, CA 94941
(415) 383-8070 or 383-4415

Southern Statuary and Stone
3401 Fifth Avenue South
Birmingham, AL 35222
(205) 322-0379 or
(800) 325-1253

Van Klassens Fine Garden
Furniture
4619B Central Avenue Road
Knoxville, TN 37912
(615) 688-2565

Winterthur Museum &
Gardens
Catalogue Division
102 Enterprise Place
Dover, DE 19735
(302) 678-9200 or
(800) 767-0500

GARDEN ORNAMENTS

The Clapper Co.
1121 Washington Street
West Newton, MA 02165
(617) 244-7900

Gardener's Eden
Box 7307
San Francisco, CA 94120-7307
(415) 428-9292 or 421-4242

Hen-Feathers & Company
10 Balligomingo Road
Gulph Mills, PA 19428
(215) 828-1721 FAX 8617

John Deere Catalog
1400 Third Avenue
Moline, IL 61265
(800) 544-2122

The Plow & Hearth
301 Madison Road
Orange, VA 22960
(703) 672-1712 or
(800) 527-5247

Reed Bros.
Turner Station
Sebastopol, CA 95472
(707) 795-6261
FAX (707)829-8620

Robinson Iron
P.O. Drawer 1235
Robinson Road
Alexander City, AL 35010
(205) 329-8486

Smith and Hawken
25 Corte Madera
Mill Valley, CA 94941
(415) 383-8070 or 383-4415

Southern Statuary and Stone
3401 Fifth Avenue South
Birmingham, AL 35222
(205) 322-0379 or
(800) 325-1253

The Well-Furnished Garden
5635 West Boulevard
Vancouver, BC,
Canada V6M 3W7
(604)263-9424 or 2601

Winterthur Museum &
Gardens
Catalogue Division
102 Enterprise Place
Dover, DE 19735
(302) 678-9200 or
(800) 767-0500

GARDEN STRUCTURES

Bow House, Inc.
P.O. Box 228
92 Randall Road
Bolton, MA 01740
(508) 779-6464

Exotic Blossoms
1533 Cherry Street
Philadelphia, PA 19102
(215) 963-9250

GAZEBOS

Cumberland Woodcraft
P.O. Drawer 609
Carlisle, PA 17013
(717) 243-0063

The Garden Concepts
Collection
P.O. Box 241233
Memphis, TN 38124-1233
(901) 756-1649

Sun Designs
P.O. Box 206
173 E. Wisconsin Avenue
(Oconomowoc)
Delafield, WI 53018-0206
(414) 567-4255

Vixen Hill Gazebos
Main Street
Elverson, PA 19520
(215) 286-0909

HAMMOCKS

Gardener's Eden
Box 7307
San Francisco, CA 94120-7307
(415) 428-9292 or 421-4242

John Deere Catalog
1400 Third Avenue
Moline, IL 61265
(800) 544-2122

LIGHT FIXTURES, OUTDOOR

Brandywine Garden Furniture
24 Phoenixville Pike
Malvern, PA 19355
(215) 640-1212 or
(800) 722-5434

Garden Magic
2001-1/2 Fairview Road
Raleigh, NC 27608
(919) 833-7315

PATIO CARTS

Brandywine Garden Furniture
24 Phoenixville Pike
Malvern, PA 19355
(215) 640-1212 or
(800) 722-5434

Reed Bros.
Turner Station
Sebastopol, CA 95472
(707) 795-6261

PLANT STANDS

The Garden Concepts
Collection
P.O. Box 241233
Memphis, TN 38124-1233
(901) 756-1649

Indoor Gardening Supplies
P.O. Box 40567
Detroit, MI 48240
(313) 668-8384

PLANTERS

Brandywine Garden Furniture
24 Phoenixville Pike
Malvern, PA 19355
(215) 640-1212 or
(800) 722-5434

Country Casual
17317 Germantown Road
Germantown, MD 20874-2999
(301) 540-0040 FAX 7364

Gardener's Eden
Box 7307
San Francisco, CA 94120-7307
(415) 428-9292 or 421-4242

Hen-Feathers & Company
10 Balligomingo Road
Gulph Mills, PA 19428
(215) 828-1721

Reed Bros.
Turner Station
Sebastopol, CA 95472
(707) 795-6261

Robinson Iron
P.O. Drawer 1235
Robinson Road
Alexander City, AL 35010
(205) 329-8486

Winterthur Museum &
Gardens
Catalogue Division
102 Enterprise Place
Dover, DE 19735
(302) 678-9200 or
(800) 767-0500

PONDS AND POOLS

Lilypons Water Gardens
P.O. Box 10
6800 Lilypons Road
Lilypons, MD 21717-0010
(301) 874-5133

Maryland Aquatic Nurseries
3427 N. Furnace Road
Jarrettsville, MD 21084
(301) 557-7615

Tilley's Nursery/The Water-
Works
111 E. Fairmount Street
Coopersburg, PA 18036
(215) 282-4784

Van Ness Water Gardens
2460 N. Euclid
Upland, CA 91786-1199
(714) 982-2425

Waterford Gardens
74 E. Allendale Road
Saddle River, NJ 07458
(201) 327-0721

Wicklein's Aquatic Farm &
Nursery, Inc.
1820 Cromwell Bridge Road
Baltimore, MD 21234
(301) 823-1335

POTTING BENCHES

Texas Greenhouse Co.
2524 White Settlement Road
Ft. Worth, TX 76107
(817) 335-5447 or
(800) 227-5447

Victory Garden Supply Co.
1428 E. High Street
Charlottesville, VA 22901
(804) 293-2298

STATUES

Hen-Feathers & Company
10 Balligomingo Road
Gulph Mills, PA 19428
(215) 828-1721

Robinson Iron
P.O. Drawer 1235
Robinson Road
Alexander City, AL 35010
(205) 329-8486

Southern Statuary and Stone
3401 Fifth Avenue South
Birmingham, AL 35222
(205) 322-0379 or
(800) 325-1253

The Well-Furnished Garden
5635 West Boulevard
Vancouver, BC,
Canada V6M 3W7
(604)263-9424

Winterthur Museum &
Gardens
Catalogue Division
102 Enterprise Place
Dover, DE 19735
(302) 678-9200 or
(800) 767-0500

SUNDIALS

Abbey Garden Sundials
P.O. Box 102
Indian Hill Road
Pakenham, ON,
Canada K0A 2X0
(613) 256-3973

American Weather Enterprises
P.O. Box 1383
Media, PA 19063
(215) 565-1232

Gardener's Eden
Box 7307
San Francisco, CA 94120-7307
(415) 428-9292 or 421-4242

Hen-Feathers & Company
10 Balligomingo Road
Gulph Mills, PA 19428
(215) 828-1721

Mrs. McGregor's Garden Shop
4801-1st Street North
Arlington, VA 22203
(703) 528-8773

The Plow & Hearth
301 Madison Road
Orange, VA 22960
(703) 672-1712 or
(800) 527-5247

The Well-Furnished Garden
5635 West Boulevard
Vancouver, BC,
Canada V6M 3W7
(604) 263-9424

SWINGS AND GLIDERS

Brandywine Garden Furniture
24 Phoenixville Pike
Malvern, PA 19355
(215) 640-1212 or
(800) 722-5434

The Clapper Co.
1121 Washington Street
West Newton, MA 02165
(617) 244-7900

Country Casual
17317 Germantown Road
Germantown, MD 20874-2999
(301) 540-0040 FAX 7364

John Deere Catalog
1400 Third Avenue
Moline, IL 61265
(800) 544-2122

TOOLS

W. Atlee Burpee Company
300 Park Avenue
Warminster, PA 18974
(215) 674-4900

Gardener's Supply Company
128 Intervale Road
Burlington, VT 05401
(802) 863-1700 or 4535

John Deere Catalog
1400 Third Avenue
Moline, IL 61265
(800) 544-2122

Kinsman Company, Inc.
River Road
Point Pleasant, PA 18950
(215) 297-5613

Langenbach Fine Tool Co.
P.O. Box 453
Blairstown, NJ 07825
(201) 362-5886

The Natural Gardening
Company
217 San Anselmo Avenue
San Anselmo, CA 94960
(415) 456-5060

Smith and Hawken
25 Corte Madera
Mill Valley, CA 94941
(415) 383-8070 or 383-4415

The Walt Nicke Company
P.O. Box 433
36 McLeod Lane
Topsfield, MA 01983
(508) 887-3388

White Flower Farm
Route 63
Litchfield, CT 06759-0050
(203) 567-0801 or
496-9600

TOPIARY FRAMES

Garden Magic
2001-1/2 Fairview Road
Raleigh, NC 27608
(919) 833-7315

TRELLISES

Cross VINYLattice
3174 Marjan Drive
Atlanta, GA 30340
(404) 451-4531

WATER GARDEN SUPPLIES

Van Ness Water Gardens
2460 N. Euclid
Upland, CA 91786-1199
(714) 982-2425

Wicklein's Aquatic Farm &
Nursery, Inc.
1820 Cromwell Bridge Road
Baltimore, MD 21234
(301) 823-1335

WEATHERVANES

American Weather Enterprises
P.O. Box 1383
Media, PA 19063
(215) 565-1232

John Deere Catalog
1400 Third Avenue
Moline, IL 61265
(800) 544-2122

Kinsman Company, Inc.
River Road
Point Pleasant, PA 18950
(215) 297-5613

Wind & Weather
P.O. Box 2320
Albion Street Watertower
Mendocino, CA 95460
(707) 937-0323

WINDOW BOXES

Kingsley-Bate, Ltd.
P.O. Box 6797
3826 S. 4 Mile Run
Arlington, VA 22206
(703) 931-9200 FAX 9201

Mrs. McGregor's Garden Shop
4801-1st Street North
Arlington, VA 22203
(703) 528-8773

INDEX

ACKNOWLEDGMENTS

The Editors wish to express special appreciation to these landscape architects and designers:

John Adams
Richard Anderson
Joe Brooks
Carter Brown
David Campbell
Heath Carrier
Shirley Carter
Robert Chesnut
Preston Dalrymple
Hugh Dargan
Mary Palmer Dargan
Edward Daugherty
Richard Dawson
Steve Dodd
Doug Dorough
Jack Douglas
Steve Dudash
Frances Durr
Edith Eddleman
Edmund Ely
Lawrence Estes
David Foresman
David Forest
Barry Fox
Dan Franklin
René Fransen
Christopher Friedrichs
Ryan Gainey
George Gambrill
Howard Garrett
Charles Godfrey
Richard Griffin
Luis A. Guevara
Beaty Hanna
Robert Hartwig
Coleman Helme
Michael Hopping
Norman Kent Johnson
Raymond Jungles
Donald Kauffmann

Henry Lambert
James Lambert
Clermont Lee
Robert Lewis
Terry Lewis
Nimrod Long
Carol Macht
Catherine Mahan
J. D. Martin
Robert Marvin
Jean Mather
William T. McDougald
Tait Moring
Don Morris
Don Nesmith
Bob Newton
Wolfgang Oehme
Ben Page
Mary Palmer
Mahlon Perry
Donnie Phillips
William Ray
Bill Rosenberg
Carolyn Sartor
Dan Sears
Bob Shaheen
Jim Sines
William T. Smith
Charles Sowell
J. Starbuck
Johnny Steele
Peter Strelkow
Fred Thode
Scott Thornton
John Troy
James Van Sweden
Fritz Von Ostoff
Sheila Wertimer
Harry White
Brian Zimmerman

COURTYARDS
To
COUNTRY GARDENS

Designed by Cynthia R. Cooper

*Text composed in Hiroshige
Book and Nuptial Script*

*Color separations by Capitol
Engraving Company,
Nashville, Tennessee*

*Printed and bound by
Ringier America,
New Berlin, Wisconsin*

*Text sheets are Multiweb Gloss
by Repap
Kimberly, Wisconsin*

*Endleaves are Kingston by
The Holliston Mills;
Rainbow Antique Mauve*

*Cover cloth is Holliston
Kingston Natural, Special
Shade by The Holliston Mills,
Kingsport, Tennessee*